Constitutional Law

EDITORIAL ADVISORS

Vicki Been
Elihu Root Professor of Law
New York University School of Law

Erwin Chemerinsky
Dean and Distinguished Professor of Law
University of California, Irvine, School of Law

Richard A. Epstein
Laurence A. Tisch Professor of Law
New York University School of Law
Peter and Kirsten Bedford Senior Fellow
The Hoover Institution
Senior Lecturer in Law
The University of Chicago

Ronald J. Gilson
Charles J. Meyers Professor of Law and Business
Stanford University
Marc and Eva Stern Professor of Law and Business
Columbia Law School

James E. Krier
Earl Warren DeLano Professor of Law
The University of Michigan Law School

Richard K. Neumann, Jr.
Professor of Law
Maurice A. Deane School of Law at Hofstra University

Robert H. Sitkoff
John L. Gray Professor of Law
Harvard Law School

David Alan Sklansky
Yosef Osheawich Professor of Law
University of California at Berkeley School of Law

Kent D. Syverud
Dean and Ethan A. H. Shepley University Professor
Washington University School of Law

2013 Supplement

Constitutional Law

Seventh Edition

Geoffrey R. Stone
Harry Kalven, Jr., Distinguished Service Professor of Law
University of Chicago Law School

Louis Michael Seidman
Carmack Waterhouse Professor of Constitutional Law
Georgetown University Law Center

Cass R. Sunstein
Felix Frankfurter Professor of Law
Harvard Law School

Mark V. Tushnet
William Nelson Cromwell Professor of Law
Harvard Law School

Pamela S. Karlan
Kenneth & Harle Montgomery Professor of Public Interest Law
Stanford Law School

Copyright © 2013 Geoffrey R. Stone; Jessica and Andrew Seidman; Cass R. Sunstein; Mark Tushnet; Pamela Karlan; and Rebecca and Laura Tushnet

Published by Wolters Kluwer Law & Business in New York.

Wolters Kluwer Law & Business serves customers worldwide with CCH, Aspen Publishers, and Kluwer Law International products. (www.wolterskluwerlb.com)

No part of this publication may be reproduced or transmitted in any form or by any means, electronic or mechanical, including photocopy, recording, or utilized by any information storage or retrieval system, without written permission from the publisher. For information about permissions or to request permissions online, visit us at www.wolterskluwerlb.com, or a written request may be faxed to our permissions department at 212-771-0803.

To contact Customer Service, e-mail customer.service@wolterskluwer.com, call 1-800-234-1660, fax 1-800-901-9075, or mail correspondence to:

> Wolters Kluwer Law & Business
> Attn: Order Department
> PO Box 990
> Frederick, MD 21705

Printed in the United States of America.

1 2 3 4 5 6 7 8 9 0

ISBN 978-1-4548-2831-0

Library of Congress Cataloging-in-Publication Data

The First Amendment / Geoffrey R. Stone ... [et al.].—4th ed.
   p. cm.—(Aspen casebook series)
  Includes index.
  ISBN 978-1-4548-0706-3 (casebook)
 1. Freedom of speech—United States. 2. Freedom of the press—United States. 3. Freedom of religion—United States. 4. United States. Constitution. 1st Amendment.
 I. Stone, Geoffrey R.
  KF4770.F558 2012
  342.7308'53—dc23

2011044674

About Wolters Kluwer Law & Business

Wolters Kluwer Law & Business is a leading global provider of intelligent information and digital solutions for legal and business professionals in key specialty areas, and respected educational resources for professors and law students. Wolters Kluwer Law & Business connects legal and business professionals as well as those in the education market with timely, specialized authoritative content and information-enabled solutions to support success through productivity, accuracy and mobility.

Serving customers worldwide, Wolters Kluwer Law & Business products include those under the Aspen Publishers, CCH, Kluwer Law International, Loislaw, ftwilliam.com and MediRegs family of products.

CCH products have been a trusted resource since 1913, and are highly regarded resources for legal, securities, antitrust and trade regulation, government contracting, banking, pension, payroll, employment and labor, and healthcare reimbursement and compliance professionals.

Aspen Publishers products provide essential information to attorneys, business professionals and law students. Written by preeminent authorities, the product line offers analytical and practical information in a range of specialty practice areas from securities law and intellectual property to mergers and acquisitions and pension/benefits. Aspen's trusted legal education resources provide professors and students with high-quality, up-to-date and effective resources for successful instruction and study in all areas of the law.

Kluwer Law International products provide the global business community with reliable international legal information in English. Legal practitioners, corporate counsel and business executives around the world rely on Kluwer Law journals, looseleafs, books, and electronic products for comprehensive information in many areas of international legal practice.

Loislaw is a comprehensive online legal research product providing legal content to law firm practitioners of various specializations. Loislaw provides attorneys with the ability to quickly and efficiently find the necessary legal information they need, when and where they need it, by facilitating access to primary law as well as state-specific law, records, forms and treatises.

ftwilliam.com offers employee benefits professionals the highest quality plan documents (retirement, welfare and non-qualified) and government forms (5500/PBGC, 1099 and IRS) software at highly competitive prices.

MediRegs products provide integrated health care compliance content and software solutions for professionals in healthcare, higher education and life sciences, including professionals in accounting, law and consulting.

Wolters Kluwer Law & Business, a division of Wolters Kluwer, is headquartered in New York. Wolters Kluwer is a market-leading global information services company focused on professionals.

Contents

Table of Cases ix
Table of Authorities xi

I. THE CONSTITUTION AND THE SUPREME COURT   1

F.   "Case or Controversy" Requirements and the Passive Virtues   1
     2.   Standing   1
         Clapper v. Amnesty Int'l USA   1

II. FEDERALISM AT WORK: CONGRESS AND THE NATIONAL ECONOMY   17

C.   The Evolution of Commerce Clause Doctrine   17
D.   State Regulation of Interstate Commerce   18
E.   Preemption   18

III. THE SCOPE OF CONGRESS'S POWERS: TAXING AND SPENDING, WAR POWERS, INDIVIDUAL RIGHTS, AND STATE AUTONOMY   19

B.   Congress's Enforcement Power under the Reconstruction Amendments   19

IV. THE DISTRIBUTION OF NATIONAL POWERS   23

C.   Foreign Affairs   23
D.   Domestic Affairs   24

V. EQUALITY AND THE CONSTITUTION — 25

C. Equal Protection Methodology: Heightened Scrutiny
and the Problem of Race — 25
    Fisher v. University of Texas — 25
E. The Problem of Sexual Orientation — 31

VI. IMPLIED FUNDAMENTAL RIGHTS — 33

F. Modern Substantive Due Process: Privacy, Personhood,
and Family — 33
    3. Family and Other Privacy Interests — 33
        United States v. Windsor — 33
H. The Contracts and Takings Clauses — 46

VII. FREEDOM OF EXPRESSION — 51

A. Introduction — 51
B. Content-Based Restrictions: Dangerous Ideas
and Information — 51
D. Content-Based Restrictions: "Low" Value — 54
E. Content-Neutral Restrictions — 57
    Agency for International Development v. Alliance for
Open Society International — 58
F. Freedom of the Press — 63

VIII. THE CONSTITUTION AND RELIGION — 65

A. Introduction: Historical and Analytical Overview — 65

IX. STATE ACTION, BASELINES, AND THE PROBLEM OF PRIVATE POWER — 67

E. Unconstitutional Conditions and the Benefit/Burden
Distinction — 67

Table of Cases

Italics indicate principal and intermediate cases.
All references are to page numbers in the main text

Abrams v. United States, 1053
Agency for International Development v. Alliance for Open Society International, 1337, 1418, 1620
Alvarez, United States v., 1263
Arizona v. United States, 290
Arkansas Game & Fish Commn. v. United States, 1003, 1013
Ashley Nicole Richards and Brent Justice, United States v., 1211
Branzburg v. Hayes, 1426
Brown v. Entertainment Merchants Association, 1214, 1263
Brown v. Socialist Workers '74 Campaign Commn., 1426
Chaplinsky v. New Hampshire, 1263
Clapper v. Amnesty Intl. USA, 106
Debs v. United States, 1052
Dolan v. City of Tigard, 1011
Federal Election Commission v. Akins, 118
Fisher v. University of Texas, 598
Frohwerk v. United States, 1052
Gratz v. Bollinger, 598
Grutter v. Bollinger, 598
Hollingsworth v. Perry, 118
Hopwood v. Texas, 598
Immigration & Naturalization Service (INS) v. Chadha, 435
Kebodeaux, United States v., 217
Koontz v. St. Johns River Water Management Dist., 1011, 1613
Lawrence v. Texas, 1201
McBurney v. Young, 263
McIntyre v. Ohio Election Commn., 1426
NAACP v. Alabama, 1426
Nollan v. California Coastal Commn., 1011, 1613
Northwestern Austin Mun. Util. Dist. No. 1 v. Holder, 335
O'Brien v. United States, 1426
Planned Parenthood of Southeastern Pennsylvania v. Casey, 1201
Regents of Univ. of Cal. v. Bakke, 598

Table of Cases

Reliable Consultants, Inc. v. Earl, 1201
Roe v. Wade, 1201
Rumsfeld v. FAIR, 1011
Schenck v. United States, 1052
Shelby County v. Holder, 335
Snyder v. Phelps, 1011, 1214, 1263
Stevens, United States v., 1211, 1214, 1263
Talley v. California, 1426
Windsor, United States v., 118, 215, 689, *937*
Windsor v. United States, 689
Yates v. United States, 1070

Table of Authorities

Abrams, Plenary Power Preemption, 99 Va. L. Rev. 601 (2013), 290
Ackerman, B., The Decline and Fall of the American Republic (2010), 423
Ashdown, Distorting Democracy: Campaign Lies in the 21st Century, 20 Wm. & Mary Bill Rts. J. 1085 (2012), 1149
Bhagwat, Details: Specific Facts and the First Amendment, 86 S. Cal. L. Rev. 1 (2012), 1112
Bradley & Morrison, Historical Gloss and the Separation of Powers, 126 Harv. L. Rev. 411 (2012), 389
Bradley & Morrison, Presidential Power, Historical Practice, and Legal Constraint, 113 Colum. L. Rev. 1097 (2013), 423
Brudney, The First Amendment and Commercial Advertising, 53 B.C. L. Rev. 1153 (2013), 1173, 1180
Coenen, Of Speech and Sanctions: Toward a Penalty-Sensitive Approach to the First Amendment, 112 Colum. L. Rev. 991 (2012), 1053
Collins, R. & Skover, D., On Dissent: Its Meaning in America (2013), 1035
Collins, Exceptional Freedom: The Roberts Court, the First Amendment, and the New Absolutism, 76 Alb. L. Rev. 409 (2013), 1263
Healy, T., The Great Dissent: How Oliver Wendell Holmes Changed His Mind—and Changed the History of Free Speech in America (2013), 1052
Heyman, To Drink the Cup of Fury: Funeral Picketing, Public Discourse, and the First Amendment, 45 Conn. L. Rev. 101 (2012), 1100
Jones, Rethinking Reporter's Privilege, 111 Mich. L. Rev. 1221 (2013), 1426
Kalven, H., A Worthy Tradition: Freedom of Speech in America (1988), 1263
Kinsley, Sexual Privacy in the Internet Age: How Substantive Due Process Protects Online Obscenity, 16 Vand. J. Ent. & Tech. L. ___ (2013), 1201
Lichman, R., The Supreme Court and McCarthy Era Repression: One Hundred Decisions (2012), 1112
Norton, The Equal Protection Implications of Government's Hateful Speech, 54 Wm. & Mary L. Rev. 159 (2012), 1334
Posner, E., & Vermeule, A., The Executive Unbound: After the Madisonian Republic (2010), 423
Schauer, Harm(s) and the First Amendment, 2011 Sup. Ct. Rev. 81, 1214
Schwartzman, What if Religion Is Not Special, 79 U. Chi. L. Rev. 1351 (2012), 1467

Siegel, the REINS Act and the Struggle to Control Agency Rulemaking, 116 N.Y.U. J. Legis. & Pub. Poly. 131 (2013), 435
Stone, G., Top Secret: When Government Keeps Us in the Dark (2007), 1426
Tarkington, A First Amendment Theory for Protecting Attorney Speech, 45 U.C. Davis L. Rev. 27 (2011), 1078

I
THE CONSTITUTION AND THE SUPREME COURT

F. "Case or Controversy" Requirements and the Passive Virtues

2. Standing

Page 106. Before the Note, add the following:

CLAPPER v. AMNESTY INT'L USA

568 U.S. ___, 133 S. Ct. 1138 (2013)

JUSTICE ALITO delivered the opinion of the Court.

Section 702 of the Foreign Intelligence Surveillance Act of 1978, 50 U.S.C. § 1881a (2006 ed., Supp. V), allows the Attorney General and the Director of National Intelligence to acquire foreign intelligence information by jointly authorizing the surveillance of individuals who are not "United States persons" and are reasonably believed to be located outside the United States. Before doing so, the Attorney General and the Director of National Intelligence normally must obtain the Foreign Intelligence Surveillance Court's approval. Respondents are United States persons whose work, they allege, requires them to engage in sensitive international communications with individuals who they believe are likely targets of surveillance under § 1881a. Respondents seek a declaration that § 1881a is unconstitutional, as well as an injunction against § 1881a-authorized surveillance. The question before us is whether respondents have Article III standing to seek this prospective relief.

Respondents assert that they can establish injury in fact because there is an objectively reasonable likelihood that their communications will be acquired under § 1881a at some point in the future. But respondents' theory of *future* injury is too speculative to satisfy the well-established requirement that threatened injury must be "certainly impending." And even if respondents could demonstrate that the threatened injury is certainly impending, they still would not be able to establish that this injury is fairly traceable to § 1881a. As an alternative argument, respondents contend that they are suffering *present* injury because the risk of § 1881a-authorized surveillance already has forced them to take costly and burdensome measures to protect the confidentiality of their international communications. But respondents cannot manufacture standing by choosing to make expenditures based on hypothetical future harm that is not certainly impending. We therefore hold that respondents lack Article III standing.

I

A...

The present case involves a constitutional challenge to § 1881a. Surveillance under § 1881a is subject to statutory conditions, judicial authorization, congressional supervision, and compliance with the Fourth Amendment. Section 1881a provides that, upon the issuance of an order from the Foreign Intelligence Surveillance Court [FISC], "the Attorney General and the Director of National Intelligence may authorize jointly, for a period of up to 1 year . . . , the targeting of persons reasonably believed to be located outside the United States to acquire foreign intelligence information." Surveillance under § 1881a may not be intentionally targeted at any person known to be in the United States or any U.S. person reasonably believed to be located abroad. Additionally, acquisitions under § 1881a must comport with the Fourth Amendment. Moreover, surveillance under § 1881a is subject to congressional oversight and several types of Executive Branch review.

Section 1881a mandates that the Government obtain the Foreign Intelligence Surveillance Court's approval of "targeting" procedures, "minimization" procedures, and a governmental certification regarding proposed surveillance. Among other things, the Government's certification must attest that (1) procedures are in place "that have been approved, have been submitted for approval, or will be submitted with the certification for approval by the [FISC] that are reasonably designed" to ensure that an acquisition is "limited to targeting persons reasonably believed to be located outside" the United States; (2) minimization procedures adequately restrict the acquisition, retention, and dissemination of nonpublic information about unconsenting U.S. persons, as appropriate; (3) guidelines have been adopted to ensure compliance with targeting limits and the Fourth Amendment; and (4) the procedures and guidelines referred to above comport with the Fourth Amendment.

The Foreign Intelligence Surveillance Court's role includes determining whether the Government's certification contains the required elements. . . .

B

Respondents are attorneys and human rights, labor, legal, and media organizations whose work allegedly requires them to engage in sensitive and sometimes privileged telephone and e-mail communications with colleagues, clients, sources, and other individuals located abroad. [Respondents] claim that they communicate by telephone and e-mail with people the Government "believes or believed to be associated with terrorist organizations," "people located in geographic areas that are a special focus" of the Government's counterterrorism or diplomatic efforts, and activists who oppose governments that are supported by the United States Government.

Respondents claim that § 1881a compromises their ability to locate witnesses, cultivate sources, obtain information, and communicate confidential information to their clients. Respondents also assert that they "have ceased engaging" in certain telephone and e-mail conversations. According to respondents, the threat of surveillance will compel them to travel abroad in order to have in-person conversations. In addition, respondents declare that they have undertaken "costly and burdensome measures" to protect the confidentiality of sensitive communications. . . .

III

A

Respondents assert that they can establish injury in fact that is fairly traceable to § 1881a because there is an objectively reasonable likelihood that their communications with their foreign contacts will be intercepted under § 1881a at some point in the future. This argument fails. . . .

[Respondents'] argument rests on their highly speculative fear that: (1) the Government will decide to target the communications of non-U.S. persons with whom they communicate; (2) in doing so, the Government will choose to invoke its authority under § 1881a rather than utilizing another method of surveillance; (3) the Article III judges who serve on the Foreign Intelligence Surveillance Court will conclude that the Government's proposed surveillance procedures satisfy § 1881a's many safeguards and are consistent with the Fourth Amendment; (4) the Government will succeed in intercepting the communications of respondents' contacts; and (5) respondents will be parties to the particular communications that the Government intercepts. . . .

[Respondents'] theory of standing, which relies on a highly attenuated chain of possibilities, does not satisfy the requirement that threatened injury must be certainly impending. Moreover, even if respondents could demonstrate injury in fact, the second link in the above-described chain of contingencies—which amounts to mere speculation about whether surveillance would be under § 1881a or some other authority—shows that respondents cannot satisfy the requirement that any injury in fact must be fairly traceable to § 1881a.

First, it is speculative whether the Government will imminently target communications to which respondents are parties. Section 1881a expressly provides that respondents, who are U.S. persons, cannot be targeted for surveillance under § 1881a. . . .

Accordingly, respondents' theory necessarily rests on their assertion that the Government will target *other individuals*—namely, their foreign contacts.

Yet respondents have no actual knowledge of the Government's § 1881a targeting practices. Instead, respondents merely speculate and make assumptions about whether their communications with their foreign contacts will be acquired under § 1881a. For example, journalist Christopher Hedges states: "I have no choice but to *assume* that any of my international communications *may* be subject to government surveillance, and I have to make decisions . . . in light of that *assumption*." Similarly, attorney Scott McKay asserts that, "[b]ecause of the [FISA Amendments Act], we now have to *assume* that every one of our international communications *may* be monitored by the government." . . .

[Because] § 1881a at most *authorizes*—but does not *mandate* or *direct*—the surveillance that respondents fear, respondents' allegations are necessarily conjectural. Simply put, respondents can only speculate as to how the Attorney General and the Director of National Intelligence will exercise their discretion in determining which communications to target.

Second, even if respondents could demonstrate that the targeting of their foreign contacts is imminent, respondents can only speculate as to whether the Government will seek to use § 1881 authorized surveillance (rather than other methods) to do so. The Government has numerous other methods of conducting surveillance, none of which is challenged here. Even after the enactment of the FISA Amendments Act, for example, the Government may still conduct electronic surveillance of persons abroad under the older provisions of FISA so long as it satisfies the applicable requirements, including a demonstration of probable cause to believe that the person is a foreign power or agent of a foreign power. The Government may also obtain information from the intelligence services of foreign nations. . . . Even if respondents could demonstrate that their foreign contacts will imminently be targeted—indeed, even if they could show that interception of their own communications will imminently occur—they would still need to show that their injury is fairly traceable to § 1881a. But, because respondents can only speculate as to whether any (asserted) interception would be under § 1881a or some other authority, they cannot satisfy the "fairly traceable" requirement.

Third, even if respondents could show that the Government will seek the Foreign Intelligence Surveillance Court's authorization to acquire the communications of respondents' foreign contacts under § 1881a, respondents can only speculate as to whether that court will authorize such surveillance. . . .

We decline to abandon our usual reluctance to endorse standing theories that rest on speculation about the decisions of independent actors. In sum, respondents' speculative chain of possibilities does not establish that injury based on potential future surveillance is certainly impending or is fairly traceable to § 1881a.

B

Respondents' alternative argument—namely, that they can establish standing based on the measures that they have undertaken to avoid § 1881a-authorized surveillance—fares no better. Respondents assert that they are suffering ongoing injuries that are fairly traceable to § 1881a because the risk of surveillance under § 1881a requires them to take costly and burdensome measures to protect the confidentiality of their communications. Respondents claim, for instance, that the threat of surveillance sometimes compels them to avoid certain e-mail and phone conversations, to "tal[k] in generalities rather than specifics," or to travel so that they can have in-person conversations. . . .

Respondents' contention that they have standing because they incurred certain costs as a reasonable reaction to a risk of harm is unavailing—because the harm respondents seek to avoid is not certainly impending. In other words, respondents cannot manufacture standing merely by inflicting harm on themselves based on their fears of hypothetical future harm that is not certainly impending. Any ongoing injuries that respondents are suffering are not fairly traceable to § 1881a.

If the law were otherwise, an enterprising plaintiff would be able to secure a lower standard for Article III standing simply by making an expenditure based on a nonparanoid fear. . . .

Thus, allowing respondents to bring this action based on costs they incurred in response to a speculative threat would be tantamount to accepting a repackaged version of respondents' first failed theory of standing.

Another reason that respondents' present injuries are not fairly traceable to § 1881a is that even before § 1881a was enacted, they had a similar incentive to engage in many of the countermeasures that they are now taking. . . .

IV

A

Respondents incorrectly maintain that "[t]he kinds of injuries incurred here—injuries incurred because of [respondents'] reasonable efforts to avoid greater injuries that are otherwise likely to flow from the conduct they challenge—are the same kinds of injuries that this Court held to support standing in cases such as" *Laidlaw* [and] Meese v. Keene, 481 U.S. 465 (1987). . . .

[Each] of these cases was very different from the present case.

In *Laidlaw*, plaintiffs' standing was based on "the proposition that a company's continuous and pervasive illegal discharges of pollutants into a river would cause nearby residents to curtail their recreational use of that waterway and would subject them to other economic and aesthetic harms." Because the unlawful discharges of pollutants were "concededly ongoing," the only issue was whether "nearby residents"—who were members of the organizational plaintiffs—acted reasonably in refraining from using the polluted area. *Laidlaw* is therefore quite unlike the present case, in which it is not "concede[d]" that respondents would be subject to unlawful surveillance but for their decision to take preventive measures. *Laidlaw* would resemble this case only if (1) it were undisputed that the Government was using § 1881a-authorized surveillance to acquire respondents' communications and (2) the sole dispute concerned the reasonableness of respondents' preventive measures.

In *Keene*, the plaintiff challenged the constitutionality of the Government's decision to label three films as "political propaganda." The Court held that the plaintiff, who was an attorney and a state legislator, had standing because he demonstrated, through "detailed affidavits," that he "could not exhibit the films without incurring a risk of injury to his reputation and of an impairment of his political career." Unlike the present case, *Keene* involved "more than a 'subjective chill'" based on speculation about potential governmental action; the plaintiff in that case was unquestionably regulated by the relevant statute, and the films that he wished to exhibit had already been labeled as "political propaganda." . . .

B

Respondents also suggest that they should be held to have standing because otherwise the constitutionality of § 1881a could not be challenged. It would be wrong, they maintain, to "insulate the government's surveillance activities from meaningful judicial review." Respondents' suggestion is both legally and factually incorrect. First, "'[t]he assumption that if respondents have no standing to sue, no one would have standing, is not a reason to find standing.'"

Second, our holding today by no means insulates § 1881a from judicial review. As described above, Congress created a comprehensive scheme in which the Foreign Intelligence Surveillance Court evaluates the Government's certifications, targeting procedures, and minimization procedures—including assessing whether the targeting and minimization procedures comport with the Fourth Amendment. Any dissatisfaction that respondents may have about the Foreign Intelligence Surveillance Court's rulings—or the congressional delineation of that court's role—is irrelevant to our standing analysis.

Additionally, if the Government intends to use or disclose information obtained or derived from a § 1881a acquisition in judicial or administrative proceedings, it must provide advance notice of its intent, and the affected person may challenge the lawfulness of the acquisition. . . .

Finally, any electronic communications service provider that the Government directs to assist in § 1881a surveillance may challenge the lawfulness of that directive before the FISC. Indeed, at the behest of a service provider, the Foreign Intelligence Surveillance Court of Review previously analyzed the constitutionality of electronic surveillance directives issued pursuant to a now-expired set of FISA amendments.

* * *

We hold that respondents lack Article III standing because they cannot demonstrate that the future injury they purportedly fear is certainly impending and because they cannot manufacture standing by incurring costs in anticipation of non-imminent harm. We therefore reverse the judgment of the Second Circuit and remand the case for further proceedings consistent with this opinion.
It is so ordered.

JUSTICE BREYER, with whom JUSTICE GINSBURG, JUSTICE SOTOMAYOR, and JUSTICE KAGAN join, dissenting.

I ...

No one here denies that the Government's interception of a private telephone or e-mail conversation amounts to an injury that is "concrete and particularized." Moreover, the plaintiffs, respondents here, seek as relief a judgment declaring unconstitutional (and enjoining enforcement of) a statutory provision authorizing those interceptions; and, such a judgment would redress the injury by preventing it. Thus, the basic question is whether the injury, *i.e.,* the interception, is "actual or imminent."

II

A ...

The addition of § 1881a in 2008 changed [prior] law in three important ways. First, it eliminated the requirement that the Government describe to the court each specific target and identify each facility at which its surveillance would be directed, thus permitting surveillance on a programmatic, not necessarily individualized, basis. Second, it eliminated the requirement that a target be a "foreign power or an agent of a foreign power." Third, it diminished the court's authority to insist upon, and eliminated its authority to supervise, instance-specific privacy-intrusion minimization procedures (though the Government still must use court-approved general minimization procedures). Thus, using the authority of § 1881a, the Government can obtain court approval for its surveillance of electronic communications between places within the United States and targets in foreign territories by showing the court (1) that "a significant purpose of the acquisition is to obtain foreign intelligence information," and (2) that it will use general targeting and privacy-intrusion minimization procedures of a kind that the court had previously approved.

B...

Plaintiff Scott McKay [says] in an affidavit (1) that he is a lawyer; (2) that he represented "Mr. Sami Omar Al-Hussayen, who was acquitted in June 2004 on terrorism charges"; (3) that he continues to represent "Mr. Al-Hussayen, who, in addition to facing criminal charges after September 11, was named as a defendant in several civil cases"; (4) that he represents Khalid Sheik Mohammed, a detainee, "before the Military Commissions at Guantanamo Bay, Cuba"; (5) that in representing these clients he "communicate[s] by telephone and email with people outside the United States, including Mr. Al-Hussayen himself," "experts, investigators, attorneys, family members . . . and others who are located abroad"; and (6) that prior to 2008 "the U.S. government had intercepted some 10,000 telephone calls and 20,000 email communications involving [his client] Al-Hussayen." . . .

[Another] plaintiff, Joanne Mariner, says in her affidavit (1) that she is a human rights researcher, (2) that "some of the work [she] do[es] involves trying to track down people who were rendered by the CIA to countries in which they were tortured"; (3) that many of those people "the CIA has said are (or were) associated with terrorist organizations"; and (4) that, to do this research, she "communicate[s] by telephone and e-mail with . . . former detainees, lawyers for detainees, relatives of detainees, political activists, journalists, and fixers" "all over the world, including in Jordan, Egypt, Pakistan, Afghanistan, [and] the Gaza Strip." . . .

III

Several considerations, based upon the record along with commonsense inferences, convince me that there is a very high likelihood that Government, *acting under the authority of* § 1881a, will intercept at least some of the communications just described. First, the plaintiffs have engaged, and continue to engage, in electronic communications of a kind that the 2008 amendment, but not the prior Act, authorizes the Government to intercept. These communications include discussions with family members of those detained at Guantanamo, friends and acquaintances of those persons, and investigators, experts and others with knowledge of circumstances related to terrorist activities. These persons are foreigners located outside the United States. They are not "foreign power[s]" or "agent[s] of . . . foreign power[s]." And the plaintiffs state that they exchange with these persons "foreign intelligence information," defined to include information that "relates to" "international terrorism" and "the national defense or the security of the United States."

Second, the plaintiffs have a strong *motive* to engage in, and the Government has a strong *motive* to listen to, conversations of the kind described. A lawyer representing a client normally seeks to learn the circumstances surrounding the crime (or the civil wrong) of which the client is accused. A fair reading of the affidavit of Scott McKay, for example, taken together with elementary considerations of a lawyer's obligation to his client, indicates that McKay will engage in conversations that concern what suspected foreign terrorists, such as his client, have done; in conversations that concern his clients' families, colleagues, and contacts; in conversations that concern what those persons (or those connected to them) have said and done, at least in relation to terrorist activities; in conversations that concern the political, social, and commercial environments in which the suspected terrorists have lived and worked; and so forth. Journalists and human rights workers have strong similar motives to conduct conversations of this kind.

At the same time, the Government has a strong motive to conduct surveillance of conversations that contain material of this kind. The Government, after all, seeks to learn as much as it can reasonably learn about suspected terrorists (such as those detained at Guantanamo), as well as about their contacts and activities, along with those of friends and family members. And the Government is motivated to do so, not simply by the desire to help convict those whom the Government believes guilty, but also by the critical, overriding need to protect America from terrorism.

Third, the Government's *past behavior* shows that it has sought, and hence will in all likelihood continue to seek, information about alleged terrorists and detainees through means that include surveillance of electronic communications. As just pointed out, plaintiff Scott McKay states that the Government (under the authority of the pre-2008 law) "intercepted some 10,000 telephone calls and 20,000 email communications involving [his client] Mr. Al-Hussayen."

Fourth, the Government has the *capacity* to conduct electronic surveillance of the kind at issue. To some degree this capacity rests upon technology available to the Government. [This] capacity also includes the Government's authority to obtain the kind of information here at issue from private carriers such as AT&T and Verizon. We are further told by *amici* that the Government is expanding that capacity.

Of course, to exercise this capacity the Government must have intelligence court authorization. But the Government rarely files requests that fail to meet the statutory criteria. As the intelligence court itself has stated, its review under § 1881a is "narrowly circumscribed." There is no reason to believe that the communications described would all fail to meet the conditions necessary for approval. Moreover, compared with prior law, § 1881a simplifies and thus expedites the approval process, making it more likely that the Government will use § 1881a to obtain the necessary approval.

The upshot is that (1) similarity of content, (2) strong motives, (3) prior behavior, and (4) capacity all point to a very strong likelihood that the Government will intercept at least some of the plaintiffs' communications, including some that the 2008 amendment, § 1881a, but not the pre-2008 Act, authorizes the Government to intercept. . . .

Consequently, we need only assume that the Government is doing its job (to find out about, and combat, terrorism) in order to conclude that there is a high probability that the Government will intercept at least some electronic communication to which at least some of the plaintiffs are parties. The majority is wrong when it describes the harm threatened plaintiffs as "speculative."

IV

A

The majority more plausibly says that the plaintiffs have failed to show that the threatened harm is "*certainly impending.*" But [*certainty*] is not, and never has been, the touchstone of standing. The future is inherently uncertain. Yet federal courts frequently entertain actions for injunctions and for declaratory relief aimed at preventing future activities that are reasonably likely or highly likely, but not absolutely certain, to take place. And that degree of certainty is all that is needed to support standing here.

The Court's use of the term "certainly impending" is not to the contrary. . . .

Taken together the case law uses the word "certainly" as if it emphasizes, rather than literally defines, the immediately following term "impending."

B
1

More important, the Court's holdings in standing cases show that standing exists here. The Court has often *found* standing where the occurrence of the relevant injury was far *less* certain than here. Consider a few, fairly typical, cases. Consider *Pennell.* A city ordinance forbade landlords to raise the rent charged to a tenant by more than 8 percent where doing so would work an unreasonably severe hardship on that tenant. A group of landlords sought a judgment declaring the ordinance unconstitutional. The Court held that, to have standing, the landlords had to demonstrate a "'*realistic danger of sustaining a direct injury* as a result of the statute's operation.'" It found that the landlords had done so by showing a likelihood of enforcement and a "probability," that the ordinance would make the landlords charge lower rents—even though the landlords had not shown (1) that they intended to raise the relevant rents to the point of causing unreasonably severe hardship; (2) that the tenants would challenge those increases; or

(3) that the city's hearing examiners and arbitrators would find against the landlords. Here, even more so than in *Pennell*, there is a *"realistic danger"* that the relevant harm will occur. . . .

How could the law be otherwise? Suppose that a federal court faced a claim by homeowners that (allegedly) unlawful dam-building practices created a high risk that their homes would be flooded. Would the court deny them standing on the ground that the risk of flood was only 60, rather than 90, percent?

Would federal courts deny standing to a plaintiff in a diversity action who claims an anticipatory breach of contract where the future breach depends on probabilities? The defendant, say, has threatened to load wheat onto a ship bound for India despite a promise to send the wheat to the United States. No one can know for certain that this will happen. Perhaps the defendant will change his mind; perhaps the ship will turn and head for the United States. Yet, despite the uncertainty, the Constitution does not prohibit a federal court from hearing such a claim. . . .

Neither do ordinary declaratory judgment actions always involve the degree of certainty upon which the Court insists here. See, *e.g.*, . . . Aetna Life Ins. Co. v. Haworth, 300 U.S. 227, 239-244 (1937).

2

In some standing cases, the Court has found that a reasonable probability of *future* injury comes accompanied with *present* injury that takes the form of reasonable efforts to mitigate the threatened effects of the future injury or to prevent it from occurring. . . .

Virtually identical circumstances are present here. Plaintiff McKay, for example, points out that, when he communicates abroad about, or in the interests of, a client (*e.g.*, a client accused of terrorism), he must "make an assessment" whether his "client's interests would be compromised" should the Government "acquire the communications." If so, he must either forgo the communication or travel abroad. . . .

4

In sum [the] word "certainly" in the phrase "certainly impending" does not refer to absolute certainty. As our case law demonstrates, what the Constitution requires is something more akin to "reasonable probability" or "high probability." The use of some such standard is all that is necessary here to ensure the actual concrete injury that the Constitution demands. The considerations set forth in Parts II and III, *supra*, make clear that the standard is readily met in this case.

* * *

While I express no view on the merits of the plaintiffs' constitutional claims, I do believe that at least some of the plaintiffs have standing to make those claims. I dissent, with respect, from the majority's contrary conclusion.

Page 118. At the end of the Note, add the following:

6. Perry *and* Windsor. The Court divided five-to-four on standing questions in two important cases involving same-sex marriage. The facts of United States v. Windsor, 570 U.S. ___ (2013), were as follows. New York recognized the marriage of Edith Windsor and Thea Spyer, who wed in Ontario, Canada in 2007. Spyer died in 2009, leaving her estate to Windsor, who sought to claim the federal estate tax exemption for surviving spouses. She was barred from doing so by section 3 of the federal Defense of Marriage Act (DOMA), which defines "marriage" and "spouse" as excluding same-sex partners. Windsor paid $363,053 in estate taxes and sought a refund, which the Internal Revenue Service denied. Windsor brought suit, objecting that DOMA is inconsistent with the Fifth Amendment.

While the case was pending, the Attorney General notified the Speaker of the House of Representatives that the Department of Justice would no longer defend the constitutionality of section 3. In response, the Bipartisan Legal Advisory Group (BLAG) of the House of Representatives sought to intervene in the litigation to defend the constitutionality of section 3. The district court allowed intervention and ruled in Windsor's favor, ordering the Treasury to refund her tax with interest. The court of appeals affirmed. Although the United States agreed with the court's conclusion, it did not comply with the judgment, but instead sought certiorari in the Supreme Court.

In an opinion by Justice Kennedy (joined by Justices Breyer, Ginsburg, Sotomayor, and Kagan), the Court held that there was no standing problem:

> In this case the United States retains a stake sufficient to support Article III jurisdiction on appeal and in proceedings before this Court. The judgment in question orders the United States to pay Windsor the refund she seeks. An order directing the Treasury to pay money is "a real and immediate economic injury," indeed as real and immediate as an order directing an individual to pay a tax. That the Executive may welcome this order to pay the refund if it is accompanied by the constitutional ruling it wants does not eliminate the injury to the national Treasury if payment is made, or to the taxpayer if it is not. The judgment orders the United States to pay money that it would not disburse but for the court's order. The Government of the United States has a valid legal argument that it is injured even if the Executive disagrees with § 3 of DOMA, which results in Windsor's liability for the tax. Windsor's ongoing claim for funds that the United States refuses to pay thus establishes a controversy sufficient for Article III jurisdiction. It would be a different case if the Executive had taken the further step of paying Windsor the refund to which she was entitled under the District Court's ruling.

The Court acknowledged that "[a] party who receives all that he has sought generally is not aggrieved by the judgment affording the relief and cannot appeal from it." But it said that this rule "does not have its source in the jurisdictional limitations of Art. III. In an appropriate case, appeal may be permitted [at] the behest of the party who has prevailed on the merits, so long as that party retains a stake in the appeal satisfying the requirements of Art. III."

The Court also noted that there was a risk that the case lacked "concrete adversariness," because the executive branch was in agreement with Windsor. It concluded, however, that this problem involved not Article III but prudential considerations, and that those considerations were not sufficient to justify a refusal to rule on the merits:

> In the case now before the Court the attorneys for BLAG present a substantial argument for the constitutionality of § 3 of DOMA. BLAG's sharp adversarial presentation of the issues satisfies the prudential concerns that otherwise might counsel against hearing an appeal from a decision with which the principal parties agree. Were this Court to hold that prudential rules require it to dismiss the case, and, in consequence, that the Court of Appeals erred in failing to dismiss it as well, extensive litigation would ensue. The district courts in 94 districts throughout the Nation would be without precedential guidance not only in tax refund suits but also in cases involving the whole of DOMA's sweep involving over 1,000 federal statutes and a myriad of federal regulations. For instance, the opinion of the Court of Appeals for the First Circuit, addressing the validity of DOMA in a case involving regulations of the Department of Health and Human Services, likely would be vacated with instructions to dismiss, its ruling and guidance also then erased. Rights and privileges of hundreds of thousands of persons would be adversely affected, pending a case in which all prudential concerns about justiciability are absent. [In] these unusual and urgent circumstances, the very term "prudential" counsels that it is a proper exercise of the Court's responsibility to take jurisdiction. For these reasons, the prudential and Article III requirements are met here; and, as a consequence, the Court need not decide whether BLAG would have standing to challenge the District Court's ruling and its affirmance in the Court of Appeals on BLAG's own authority.

Justice Scalia (joined by Chief Justice Roberts and Justice Thomas) dissented. He wrote that "the plaintiff and the Government agree entirely on what should happen in this lawsuit. They agree that the court below got it right; and they agreed in the court below that the court below that one got it right as well. What, then, are we *doing* here?" He added:

What the petitioner United States asks us to do in the case before us is exactly what the respondent Windsor asks us to do: not to provide relief from the judgment below but to say that that judgment was correct. And the same was true in the Court of Appeals: Neither party sought to undo the judgment for Windsor, and so that court should have dismissed the appeal (just as we should dismiss) for lack of jurisdiction. Since both parties agreed with the judgment of the District Court for the Southern District of New York, the suit should have ended there. The further proceedings have been a contrivance, having no object in mind except to elevate a District Court judgment that has no precedential effect in other courts, to one that has precedential effect throughout the Second Circuit, and then (in this Court) precedential effect throughout the United States.

In a separate dissenting opinion, Justice Alito essentially agreed with Justice Scalia with respect to the United States, but concluded that "the House of Representatives, which has authorized BLAG to represent its interests in this matter," suffered injury in fact, because the adverse decision had injured its ability to legislate. "In the narrow category of cases in which a court strikes down an Act of Congress and the Executive declines to defend the Act, Congress both has standing to defend the undefended statute and is a proper party to do so."

Having disposed of the standing issue, the Court reached the merits and held that DOMA was unconstitutional. This aspect of the case is considered in Chapter VI F 3 of this Supplement.

In Hollingsworth v. Perry, ___ U.S. ___ (2013), the merits involved the constitutionality of a ballot initiative known as Proposition 8, which amended the California Constitution to define marriage as a union between a man and a woman. Same-sex couples, seeking to marry, filed suit in federal court, challenging Proposition 8 under the Fourteenth Amendment. After California officials (the named defendants) refused to defend the law, the district court allowed the initiative's official proponents to intervene to defend it. After a trial, the court declared Proposition 8 unconstitutional and enjoined public officials from enforcing it. Those officials elected not to appeal, but the proponents did so. The court of appeals certified to the California Supreme Court the question whether official proponents of a ballot initiative have authority to assert the State's interest in defending the constitutionality of the initiative when public officials refuse to do so. The California Supreme Court answered that they did.

Notwithstanding that answer, the Court concluded that the requirements of Article III were not met. Chief Justice Roberts (joined by Justices Scalia, Ginsburg, Breyer, and Kagan) explained that the proponents of the law had only a generalized grievance and no "direct stake" in the case. "Their only interest in having the District Court order reversed was to vindicate the constitutional validity of a generally applicable California law." To be sure, the proponents of a ballot proposition have a particular interest under California law, "but only when it comes to the process of enacting the law." After enactment, they "have no 'personal stake' in defending its enforcement that is distinguishable from the general interest of every citizen of California."

The Court acknowledged the proponents' argument that "even if they have no cognizable interest in appealing the District Court's judgment, the State of California does, and they may assert that interest on the State's behalf." But the Court responded that it is "a 'fundamental restriction on our authority' that '[i]n the ordinary course, a litigant must assert his or her own legal rights and interests, and cannot rest a claim to relief on the legal rights or interests of third parties.'" Exceptions to that presumption could not be found here. To the argument that California itself recognized a right here, the Court said that "no matter its reasons, the fact that a State thinks a private party should have standing to seek relief for a generalized grievance cannot override our settled law to the contrary. [We] have never before upheld the standing of a private party to defend the constitutionality of a state statute when state officials have chosen not to. We decline to do so for the first time here."

In dissent, Justice Kennedy (writing for himself and for Justices Thomas, Alito, and Sotomayor), emphasized that "[under] California law, a proponent has the authority to appear in court and assert the State's interest in defending an enacted initiative when the public officials charged with that duty refuse to do so." In his view, that authority is akin to a property right, one that gives rise to injury in fact. "Proponents' authority under state law is not a contrivance. It is not a fictional construct. It is the product of the California Constitution and the California Elections Code." As a matter of state law, the purpose of the initiative process "is undermined if the very officials the initiative process seeks to circumvent are the only parties who can defend an enacted initiative when it is challenged in a legal proceeding."

Is the Court's majority saying that a state lacks the constitutional power to create a legal right to defend the outcome of a referendum? If so, how is its decision consistent with *Akins*? Is *Windsor* consistent with *Perry*?

II
FEDERALISM AT WORK: CONGRESS AND THE NATIONAL ECONOMY

C. The Evolution of the Commerce Clause Doctrine

Page 215. At the end of section 1 of the Note, add the following:

(In United States v. Windsor, 570 U.S. ___ (2013), Justice Kennedy's opinion for the Court observed that the Defense of Marriage Act, held unconstitutional on equal protection grounds, was "an unusual deviation from the usual tradition of recognizing and accepting state definitions of marriage[, which] is strong evidence of a law having the purpose and effect of disapproval of that class." That "purpose and effect" were what rendered the statute unconstitutional as a violation of equality. *Windsor* is excerpted at greater length in Chapter VI F 3 of this Supplement.)

Page 217. At the end of section 4 of the Note, add the following:

For additional discussion of the necessary and proper clause, see United States v. Kebodeaux, 570 U.S. ___ (2013).

D. State Regulation of Interstate Commerce

Page 263. At the end of section 2 of the Note, add the following:

e. For a recent discussion of the privileges and immunities clause and the dormant commerce clause, see McBurney v. Young, ___ U.S. ___ 133 S. Ct. 1709 (2013), holding that a Virginia freedom of information statute limiting its use to state citizens is constitutional. According to the Court, statutory access to state-held information is not a "fundamental" right protected by the privileges and immunities clause, the distinction was not drawn to provide economic protection to citizens engaged in businesses using state-held information, and Virginia provided reasonable alternative methods by which out-of-state citizens could get access to information about judicial and other public proceedings. Questioning whether the statute triggered dormant commerce clause scrutiny (because the statute did not prohibit access to an interstate market or unduly burden such access), the Court held that the market-participant doctrine permitted the distinction because the state had created the market for information subject to the freedom of information act.

E. Preemption

Page 290. At the end of section 7 of the Note, add the following:

For an argument that *Arizona v. United States* exemplifies a distinctive form of "plenary power preemption," see Abrams, Plenary Power Preemption, 99 Va. L. Rev. 601 (2013). What subjects might be covered by such a doctrine, in addition to immigration/alienage and foreign affairs? In what sense is national power over such subjects "plenary" while national power over interstate commerce is not? How might "plenary power preemption" differ from "field preemption"?

III
THE SCOPE OF CONGRESS'S POWERS: TAXING AND SPENDING, WAR POWERS, INDIVIDUAL RIGHTS, AND STATE AUTONOMY

B. Congress's Enforcement Powers under the Reconstruction Amendments

Page 335. After section 3 of the Note, add the following:

3a. *Justifying "current burdens" by "current needs."* The Voting Rights Act of 1965 (VRA) adopted an aggressive remedy for protection of voting rights. Section 4 of the Act provided a "coverage formula" that singled out several states and political subdivisions that used literacy tests or similar devices as a prerequisite to voting and where registration or turnout in the 1964 election was significantly below the national average. The formula was amended in 1970 and 1975 to cover jurisdictions with low participation in either or both the 1968 or 1972 election. Those covered jurisdictions were required, under section 5 of the Act, to obtain federal approval before making changes in their voting laws. In 1982 and 2006, Congress extended section 5's "preclearance requirement" without changing the coverage formula.

In Shelby County v. Holder, ___ U.S. ___ (2013), the Supreme Court, in an opinion by Chief Justice Roterts, held that the coverage formula of section 4 was unconstitutional and could no longer be used to subject jurisdictions to the preclearance regime of section 5.

Referring to its decision in Northwest Austin Mun. Util. Dist. No. 1 v. Holder, 557 U.S. 193 (2009), the Court emphasized that "the Act imposes current burdens and must be justified by current needs." It saw the Act's preclearance regime as a departure from baseline constitutional principles because the Act "suspends 'all changes to state election law'—however innocuous—until they have been pre-cleared by federal authorities in Washington, D.C.," requiring states to "beseech the Federal Government for permission to implement laws that they would otherwise have the right to enact and execute on their own," and because, "despite the tradition of equal sovereignty, the Act applies to only nine States (and several additional counties)." While "these departures from the basic features of our system of government" may have been justified by the pervasive discrimination that existed in 1965, they were no longer justified: "Nearly 50 years later, things have changed dramatically":

> When upholding the constitutionality of the coverage formula in 1966, we concluded that it was "rational in both practice and theory." The formula looked to cause (discriminatory tests) and effect (low voter registration and turnout), and tailored the remedy (preclearance) to those jurisdictions exhibiting both.
>
> By 2009, however, we concluded that the "coverage formula raise[d] serious constitutional questions." As we explained, a statute's "current burdens" must be justified by "current needs," and any "disparate geographic coverage" must be "sufficiently related to the problem that it targets." The coverage formula met that test in 1965, but no longer does so.
>
> Coverage today is based on decades-old data and eradicated practices. The formula captures States by reference to literacy tests and low voter registration and turnout in the 1960s and early 1970s. But such tests have been banned nationwide for over 40 years. And voter registration and turnout numbers in the covered States have risen dramatically in the years since. Racial disparity in those numbers was compelling evidence justifying the preclearance remedy and the coverage formula. There is no longer such a disparity.
>
> In 1965, the States could be divided into two groups: those with a recent history of voting tests and low voter registration and turnout, and those without those characteristics. Congress based its coverage formula on that distinction. Today the Nation is no longer divided along those lines, yet the Voting Rights Act continues to treat it as if it were.

Justice Ginsburg, joined by Justices Breyer, Sotomayor, and Kagan, dissented. Their view was that Congress, rather than the Court, should decide whether the coverage formula remains appropriate:

III. The Scope of Congress's Powers

It is well established that Congress' judgment regarding exercise of its power to enforce the Fourteenth and Fifteenth Amendments warrants substantial deference. The VRA addresses the combination of race discrimination and the right to vote, which is "preservative of all rights." Yick Wo v. Hopkins, 118 U.S. 356, 370 (1886). When confronting the most constitutionally invidious form of discrimination, and the most fundamental right in our democratic system, Congress' power to act is at its height.

The basis for this deference is firmly rooted in both constitutional text and precedent. The Fifteenth Amendment, which targets precisely and only racial discrimination in voting rights, states that, in this domain, "Congress shall have power to enforce this article by appropriate legislation." . . .

It cannot tenably be maintained that the VRA, an Act of Congress adopted to shield the right to vote from racial discrimination, is inconsistent with the letter or spirit of the Fifteenth Amendment, or any provision of the Constitution read in light of the Civil War Amendments. Nowhere in today's opinion [is] there clear recognition of the transformative effect the Fifteenth Amendment aimed to achieve. . . .

The stated purpose of the Civil War Amendments was to arm Congress with the power and authority to protect all persons within the Nation from violations of their rights by the States. In exercising that power, then, Congress may use "all means which are appropriate, which are plainly adapted" to the constitutional ends declared by these Amendments. McCulloch, 4 Wheat., at 421. So when Congress acts to enforce the right to vote free from racial discrimination, we ask not whether Congress has chosen the means most wise, but whether Congress has rationally selected means appropriate to a legitimate end. "It is not for us to review the congressional resolution of [the need for its chosen remedy]. It is enough that we be able to perceive a basis upon which the Congress might resolve the conflict as it did." Katzenbach v. Morgan, 384 U.S. 641, 653 (1966). . . .

For three reasons, legislation reauthorizing an existing statute is especially likely to satisfy the minimal requirements of the rational-basis test. First, when reauthorization is at issue, Congress has already assembled a legislative record justifying the initial legislation. Congress is entitled to consider that preexisting record as well as the record before it at the time of the vote on reauthorization. . . .

Second, the very fact that reauthorization is necessary arises because Congress has built a temporal limitation into the Act. . . .

Third, a reviewing court should expect the record supporting reauthorization to be less stark than the record originally made. Demand for a record of violations equivalent to the one earlier made would expose Congress to a catch-22. If the statute was working, there would be less evidence of discrimination, so opponents might argue that Congress should not be allowed to renew the statute. In contrast, if the statute was not working, there would be plenty of evidence of discrimination, but scant reason to renew a failed regulatory regime.

IV
THE DISTRIBUTION OF NATIONAL POWERS

C. Foreign Affairs

Page 389.   At the end of section 2 of the Note, add the following:

Consider also Bradley & Morrison, Historical Gloss and the Separation of Powers, 126 Harv. L. Rev. 411, 414-415 (2012):

> [The] concept of institutional acquiescence needs to be tied more closely to the reality of how the political branches actually interact. Claims about acquiescence are typically based on a Madisonian conception of interbranch competition pursuant to which Congress and the Executive are each assumed to have the tools and motivation to guard against encroachments on their authority. It has become apparent from political science scholarship, however, that the Madisonian model does not accurately reflect the dynamics of modern congressional-executive relations. [Although] Congress and the President may disagree about particular policies, Congress as a body does not systematically seek to protect its prerogatives against presidential encroachment.

Bradley and Morrison conclude that this fact argues "not so much for rejecting the idea of acquiescence altogether as for being more cautious about treating apparently legislative inaction as acquiescence, and for looking beyond formal enactments when assessing whether any given case actually involves acquiescence

Page 389   **IV. The Distribution of National Powers**

or nonacquiescence." In particular, a finding of acquiescence may be more defensible "when the practice in question is not only long standing but also the product of bipartisan choices." Id.

D. Domestic Affairs

Page 423. After the first paragraph of section 3 of the Note, add the following:

For a discussion of the extent to which, and methods by which, the president is controlled by law rather than politics, see Bradley & Morrison, Presidential Power, Historical Practice, and Legal Constraint, 113 Colum. L. Rev. 1097 (2013). For arguments that legal constraints on the executive have mostly collapsed, see B. Ackerman, The Decline and Fall of the American Republic (2010); E. Posner & A. Vermeule, The Executive Unbound: After the Madisonian Republic (2010).

Page 435. At the end of section 1 of the Note, add the following:

Consider the "Regulation from the Executive in Need of Scrutiny Act of 2011," passed by the House of Representatives in 2011, REINS Act, H.R. 10, 112th Cong., § 3, which provides that a "major rule [promulgated by an administrative agency] shall not take effect unless the Congress enacts a joint resolution of approval." The Senate has not passed the Act. If it were enacted into law, would it be constitutional? Compare Statement of Rep. John Conyers, Jr., Ranking Member, H. Comm. on the Judiciary, REINS Act—Promoting Jobs and Expanding Freedom by Reducing Needless Regulations: Hearings Before the Subcomm. on Courts, Commercial & Admin. Law of the H. Comm. on the Judiciary, 112th Cong. 8 (2011) (arguing that the Act would violate *Chadha* because if an agency promulgated a rule, either House of Congress acting alone could block it by not passing a resolution of approval) with Siegel, The REINS Act and the Struggle to Control Agency Rulemaking, 16 N.Y.U. J. Legis. & Pub. Pol'y 131, 185 (2013) (arguing that the Act is "a bad idea" because Congress lacks the time and expertise to decide these questions but that it is "perfectly constitutional" because it "merely reclaim[s] the power that Congress has ceded over time").

V

EQUALITY AND THE CONSTITUTION

C. *Equal Protection Methodology: Heightened Scrutiny and the Problem of Race*

Page 598. At the end of the page, add the following:

Has the Supreme Court tightened up the narrow tailoring requirement announced in *Grutter*?

FISHER v. UNIVERSITY OF TEXAS, ___ U.S. ___ (2013). After the Fifth Circuit held in Hopwood v. Texas, 78 F.3d 932 (1996), that the University of Texas's consideration of race in its admissions process violated the equal protection clause because it did not further a compelling government interest, the Texas legislature adopted a measure known as the Top Ten Percent Law. That statute granted automatic admission to the University (as well as other public institutions) to all students from Texas high schools who are in the top 10% of their class. Following the Supreme Court's decision in Grutter v. Bollinger, 539 U.S. 306 (2003), holding that racial diversity can be a compelling government interest, the University adopted an additional admissions program in which race was one factor taken into account in admitting the portion of the entering class that was not admitted under the Top Ten Percent Law.

Alison Fisher, a white student who had been denied admission to the University, brought suit, alleging that the University's consideration of race violated the equal protection clause. The district court and the court of appeals ruled in favor of the University, holding that the University was entitled to substantial deference both in deciding that racial diversity was a compelling state interest and in deciding how to achieve that diversity.

The Supreme Court, in an opinion by Justice Kennedy, reversed, holding that the court of appeals had not applied "the correct standard of strict scrutiny." The Court took as given its prior decisions in Regents of Univ. of Cal. v. Bakke, 438 U.S. 265 (1978); *Grutter*; and Gratz v. Bollinger, 539 U.S. 244 (2003), which had found that "the interest in the educational benefits that flow from a diverse student body" was "one compelling interest that could justify the consideration of race."

"Once the University has established that its goal of diversity is consistent with strict scrutiny, however, there must still be a further judicial determination that the admissions process meets strict scrutiny in its implementation. The University must prove that the means chosen by the University to attain diversity are narrowly tailored to that goal. On this point, the University receives no deference. *Grutter* made clear that it is for the courts, not for university administrators, to ensure that '[t]he means chosen to accomplish the [government's] asserted purpose must be specifically and narrowly framed to accomplish that purpose.' True, a court can take account of a university's experience and expertise in adopting or rejecting certain admissions processes. But, as the Court said in *Grutter*, it remains at all times the University's obligation to demonstrate, and the Judiciary's obligation to determine, that admissions processes 'ensure that each applicant is evaluated as an individual and not in a way that makes an applicant's race or ethnicity the defining feature of his or her application.'

"Narrow tailoring also requires that the reviewing court verify that it is 'necessary' for a university to use race to achieve the educational benefits of diversity. *Bakke*. This involves a careful judicial inquiry into whether a university could achieve sufficient diversity without using racial classifications. Although '[n]arrow tailoring does not require exhaustion of every conceivable race-neutral alternative,' strict scrutiny does require a court to examine with care, and not defer to, a university's 'serious, good faith consideration of workable race-neutral alternatives.' See *Grutter*. Consideration by the university is of course necessary, but it is not sufficient to satisfy strict scrutiny: The reviewing court must ultimately be satisfied that no workable race-neutral alternatives would produce the educational benefits of diversity. If '"a nonracial approach . . . could promote the substantial interest about as well and at tolerable administrative expense,"' Wygant v. Jackson Bd. of Ed., 476 U.S. 267, 280, n.6 (1986) (quoting Greenawalt, Judicial Scrutiny of "Benign" Racial Preference in Law School Admissions, 75 Colum. L. Rev. 559, 578-579 (1975)), then the university may not consider race. A plaintiff, of course, bears the burden of placing the validity of a university's adoption of an affirmative action plan in issue. But strict scrutiny imposes on the university the ultimate burden of demonstrating, before turning to racial classifications, that available, workable race-neutral alternatives do not suffice."

V. Equality and the Constitution

Because the court of appeals had instead presumed that the University's decision to reintroduce race as an admissions factor was permissible, the Supreme Court remanded the case "so that the admissions process can be considered and judged under a correct analysis."

Justice Scalia wrote a short concurring opinion adhering to the view he expressed in *Grutter* that the Fourteenth Amendment "proscribes government discrimination on the basis of race, and state-provided education is no exception," but noting that because Fisher had not asked the Court to overrule *Grutter*, he joined the Court's opinion.

Justice Thomas wrote a lengthier concurrence, taking the position that "a State's use of race in higher education admissions decisions is categorically prohibited by the Equal Protection Clause." He saw "nothing 'pressing' or 'necessary' about obtaining whatever educational benefits may flow from racial diversity":

"[T]he educational benefits flowing from student body diversity—assuming they exist—hardly qualify as a compelling state interest. Indeed, the argument that educational benefits justify racial discrimination was advanced in support of racial segregation in the 1950's, but emphatically rejected by this Court. And just as the alleged educational benefits of segregation were insufficient to justify racial discrimination then, see Brown v. Board of Education, 347 U.S. 483 (1954), the alleged educational benefits of diversity cannot justify racial discrimination today."

He then drew a series of parallels between the arguments advanced by the University and the arguments that had been advanced in favor of racial segregation:

"The University asserts, for instance, that the diversity obtained through its discriminatory admissions program prepares its students to become leaders in a diverse society. See, e.g., Brief for Respondents 6 (arguing that student body diversity 'prepares students to become the next generation of leaders in an increasingly diverse society'). The segregationists likewise defended segregation on the ground that it provided more leadership opportunities for blacks. See, e.g., Brief for Respondents in Sweatt 96 ('[A] very large group of Northern Negroes [comes] South to attend separate colleges, suggesting that the Negro does not secure as well-rounded a college life at a mixed college, and that the separate college offers him positive advantages; that there is a more normal social life for the Negro in a separate college; that there is a greater opportunity for full participation and for the development of leadership; that the Negro is inwardly more "secure" at a college of his own people'); Brief for Appellees in Davis 25-26 ('The Negro child gets an opportunity to participate in segregated schools that I have never seen accorded to him in non-segregated schools. He is important, he holds offices, he is accepted by his fellows, he is on athletic teams, he has a full place there' (internal quotation marks omitted)). This argument was unavailing. It is irrelevant under the Fourteenth Amendment whether segregated or mixed schools produce better leaders. Indeed, no court today would accept the suggestion that segregation is permissible because historically black colleges produced Booker T. Washington, Thurgood Marshall, Martin Luther King, Jr., and other prominent leaders. Likewise, the University's racial discrimination cannot be justified on the ground that it will produce better leaders.

"The University also asserts that student body diversity improves interracial relations. See, e.g., Brief for Respondents 6 (arguing that student body diversity promotes 'cross-racial understanding' and breaks down racial and ethnic stereotypes). In this argument, too, the University repeats arguments once marshaled in support of segregation. See, e.g., Brief for Appellees in Davis 17 ('Virginia has established segregation in certain fields as a part of her public policy to prevent violence and reduce resentment. The result, in the view of an overwhelming Virginia majority, has been to improve the relationship between the different races'); id., at 25 ('If segregation be stricken down, the general welfare will be definitely harmed . . . there would be more friction developed' (internal quotation marks omitted)); Brief for Respondents in Sweatt 93 ('Texas has had no serious breaches of the peace in recent years in connection with its schools. The separation of the races has kept the conflicts at a minimum'); id., at 97-98 ('The legislative acts are based not only on the belief that it is the best way to provide education for both races, and the knowledge that separate schools are necessary to keep public support for the public schools, but upon the necessity to maintain the public peace, harmony, and welfare'); Brief for Appellees in Briggs 32 ('The southern Negro, by and large, does not want an end to segregation in itself any more than does the southern white man. The Negro in the South knows that discriminations, and worse, can and would multiply in such event' (internal quotation marks omitted)). We flatly rejected this line of arguments in McLaurin v. Oklahoma State Regents for Higher Ed., 339 U.S. 637 (1950), where we held that segregation would be unconstitutional even if white students never tolerated blacks. Id., at 641 ('It may be argued that appellant will be in no better position when these restrictions are removed, for he may still be set apart by his fellow students. This we think irrelevant. There is a vast difference—a Constitutional difference—between restrictions imposed by the state which prohibit the intellectual commingling of students, and the refusal of individuals to commingle where the state presents no such bar'). It is, thus, entirely irrelevant whether the University's racial discrimination increases or decreases tolerance.

"Finally, while the University admits that racial discrimination in admissions is not ideal, it asserts that it is a temporary necessity because of the enduring race consciousness of our society. See Brief for Respondents 53-54 ('Certainly all aspire for a colorblind society in which race does not matter. . . . But in Texas, as in America, "our highest aspirations are yet unfulfilled"'). Yet again, the University echoes the hollow justifications advanced by the segregationists. See, e.g., Brief for State of Kansas on Reargument in Brown v. Board of Education, O.T. 1953, No. 1, p. 56 ('We grant that segregation may not be the ethical or political ideal. At the same time we recognize that practical considerations may prevent realization of the ideal'); Brief for Respondents in Sweatt 94 ('The racial consciousness and feeling which exists today in the minds of many people may be regrettable and unjustified. Yet they are a reality which must be dealt with by the State if it is to preserve harmony and peace and at the same time furnish equal education to both groups'); id., at 96 ('"[T]he mores of racial relationships are such as to rule out, for the present at least, any possibility of admitting white persons and Negroes to the same institutions"'); Brief for Appellees in Briggs 26-27 ('[I]t would be unwise in administrative practice . . . to mix the two races in the same schools at the present time and under present conditions'); Brief for Appellees on Reargument in Briggs v. Elliott, O.T. 1953, No. 2, p. 79 ('It is not "racism" to be cognizant of the fact that mankind has struggled with race problems and racial tensions for upwards of sixty centuries'). But these arguments too were unavailing. The Fourteenth Amendment views racial bigotry as an evil to be stamped out, not as an excuse for perpetual racial tinkering by the State. See DeFunis v. Odegaard, 416 U.S. 312, 342 (1974) (Douglas, J., dissenting) ('The Equal Protection Clause commands the elimination of racial barriers, not their creation in order to satisfy our theory as to how society ought to be organized'). The University's arguments to this effect are similarly insufficient to justify discrimination. . . .

"The worst forms of racial discrimination in this Nation have always been accompanied by straight-faced representations that discrimination helped minorities.

"Slaveholders argued that slavery was a 'positive good' that civilized blacks and elevated them in every dimension of life. . . .

"A century later, segregationists similarly asserted that segregation was not only benign, but good for black students. They argued, for example, that separate schools protected black children from racist white students and teachers. . . .

"Following in these inauspicious footsteps, the University would have us believe that its discrimination is likewise benign. I think the lesson of history is clear enough: Racial discrimination is never benign. . . .

"While it does not, for constitutional purposes, matter whether the University's racial discrimination is benign, I note that racial engineering does in fact have insidious consequences. There can be no doubt that the University's discrimination injures white and Asian applicants who are denied admission because of their race. But I believe the injury to those admitted under the University's discriminatory admissions program is even more harmful.

"Blacks and Hispanics admitted to the University as a result of racial discrimination are, on average, far less prepared than their white and Asian classmates. In the University's entering class of 2009, for example, among the students admitted outside the Top Ten Percent plan, blacks scored at the 52d percentile of 2009 SAT takers nationwide, while Asians scored at the 93d percentile. Blacks had a mean

GPA of 2.57 and a mean SAT score of 1524; Hispanics had a mean GPA of 2.83 and a mean SAT score of 1794; whites had a mean GPA of 3.04 and a mean SAT score of 1914; and Asians had a mean GPA of 3.07 and a mean SAT score of 1991....

"The University admits minorities who otherwise would have attended less selective colleges where they would have been more evenly matched. But, as a result of the mismatching, many blacks and Hispanics who likely would have excelled at less elite schools are placed in a position where underperformance is all but inevitable because they are less academically prepared than the white and Asian students with whom they must compete. Setting aside the damage wreaked upon the self-confidence of these overmatched students, there is no evidence that they learn more at the University than they would have learned at other schools for which they were better prepared. Indeed, they may learn less....

"[T]hese students may well drift towards less competitive majors because the mismatch caused by racial discrimination in admissions makes it difficult for them to compete in more rigorous majors.

"Moreover, the University's discrimination 'stamp[s] [blacks and Hispanics] with a badge of inferiority.' *Adarand*, 515 U.S., at 241 (opinion of Thomas, J.). It taints the accomplishments of all those who are admitted as a result of racial discrimination. Cf. J. McWhorter, Losing the Race: Self-Sabotage in Black America 248 (2000) ('I was never able to be as proud of getting into Stanford as my classmates could be. . . . [H]ow much of an achievement can I truly say it was to have been a good enough black person to be admitted, while my colleagues had been considered good enough people to be admitted'). And, it taints the accomplishments of all those who are the same race as those admitted as a result of racial discrimination. In this case, for example, most blacks and Hispanics attending the University were admitted without discrimination under the Top Ten Percent plan, but no one can distinguish those students from the ones whose race played a role in their admission...."

Justice Ginsburg issued a short dissent, stating that she would have upheld the University's admissions policy:

"Petitioner urges that Texas' Top Ten Percent Law and race-blind holistic review of each application achieve significant diversity, so the University must be content with those alternatives. I have said before and reiterate here that only an ostrich could regard the supposedly neutral alternatives as race unconscious. See *Gratz*, 539 U.S., at 303-304, n.10 (dissenting opinion). As Justice Souter observed, the vaunted alternatives suffer from 'the disadvantage of deliberate obfuscation.' Id., at 297-298 (dissenting opinion).

"Texas' percentage plan was adopted with racially segregated neighborhoods and schools front and center stage...." In a footnote, she added that "[t]he notion that Texas' Top Ten Percent Law is race neutral calls to mind Professor Thomas Reed Powell's famous statement: 'If you think that you can think about a thing inextricably attached to something else without thinking of the thing which it is

V. Equality and the Constitution

attached to, then you have a legal mind.' T. Arnold, The Symbols of Government 101 (1935) (internal quotation marks omitted). Only that kind of legal mind could conclude that an admissions plan specifically designed to produce racial diversity is not race conscious."

"Among constitutionally permissible options, I remain convinced, 'those that candidly disclose their consideration of race [are] preferable to those that conceal it.' *Gratz*, 539 U.S., at 305, n.11 (dissenting opinion).

"Accordingly, I would not return this case for a second look. . . ."

Justice Kagan did not participate.

E. *The Problem of Sexual Orientation*

Page 689. At the end of the block quote, add the following:

The Supreme Court affirmed *Windsor* in United States v. Windsor, 570 U.S. ___ (2013). The opinions in the case are excerpted in Chapter VI F 3 of this Supplement. Justice Kennedy, writing for the Court's majority, stated that "[t]he liberty protected by the Fifth Amendment's Due Process Clause contains within it the prohibition against denying to any person the equal protection of the laws. While the Fifth Amendment itself withdraws from Government the power to degrade or demean in the way this law does, the equal protection guarantee of the Fourteenth Amendment makes that Fifth Amendment right all the more specific and all the better understood and preserved." The majority opinion does not discuss the appropriate standard of review. Consider the following excerpt from Justice Alito's dissenting opinion:

> Our equal protection framework, upon which Windsor and the United States rely, is a judicial construct that provides a useful mechanism for analyzing a certain universe of equal protection cases. But that framework is ill suited for use in evaluating the constitutionality of laws based on the traditional understanding of marriage, which fundamentally turn on what marriage is. . . .
>
> In asking the Court to determine that § 3 of DOMA is subject to and violates heightened scrutiny, Windsor and the United States thus ask us to rule that the presence of two members of the opposite sex is as rationally related to marriage as white skin is to voting or a Y-chromosome is to the ability to administer an estate. That is a striking request and one that unelected judges should pause before granting. Acceptance of the argument would cast all those who cling to traditional beliefs about the nature of marriage in the role of bigots or superstitious fools.

By asking the Court to strike down DOMA as not satisfying some form of heightened scrutiny, Windsor and the United States are really seeking to have the Court resolve a debate between two competing views of marriage.

The first and older view, which I will call the "traditional" or "conjugal" view, sees marriage as an intrinsically opposite-sex institution. BLAG notes that virtually every culture, including many not influenced by the Abrahamic religions, has limited marriage to people of the opposite sex. And BLAG attempts to explain this phenomenon by arguing that the institution of marriage was created for the purpose of channeling heterosexual intercourse into a structure that supports child rearing. Others explain the basis for the institution in more philosophical terms. They argue that marriage is essentially the solemnizing of a comprehensive, exclusive, permanent union that is intrinsically ordered to producing new life, even if it does not always do so. While modern cultural changes have weakened the link between marriage and procreation in the popular mind, there is no doubt that, throughout human history and across many cultures, marriage has been viewed as an exclusively opposite-sex institution and as one inextricably linked to procreation and biological kinship.

The other, newer view is what I will call the "consent-based" vision of marriage, a vision that primarily defines marriage as the solemnization of mutual commitment—marked by strong emotional attachment and sexual attraction—between two persons. At least as it applies to heterosexual couples, this view of marriage now plays a very prominent role in the popular understanding of the institution. Indeed, our popular culture is infused with this understanding of marriage. Proponents of same-sex marriage argue that because gender differentiation is not relevant to this vision, the exclusion of same-sex couples from the institution of marriage is rank discrimination.

The Constitution does not codify either of these views of marriage (although I suspect it would have been hard at the time of the adoption of the Constitution or the Fifth Amendment to find Americans who did not take the traditional view for granted). The silence of the Constitution on this question should be enough to end the matter as far as the judiciary is concerned. Yet, Windsor and the United States implicitly ask us to endorse the consent-based view of marriage and to reject the traditional view, thereby arrogating to ourselves the power to decide a question that philosophers, historians, social scientists, and theologians are better qualified to explore. Because our constitutional order assigns the resolution of questions of this nature to the people, I would not presume to enshrine either vision of marriage in our constitutional jurisprudence....

VI
IMPLIED FUNDAMENTAL RIGHTS

F. *Modern Substantive Due Process: Privacy, Personhood, and Family*

3. Family and Other Privacy Interests

Page 937. At the end of the Note, add the following:

UNITED STATES v. WINDSOR

570 U.S. ___ (2013)

JUSTICE KENNEDY delivered the opinion of the Court.

I

[Section 3 of the Defense of Marriage Act, 1 U.S.C. § 7 (DOMA) provides:

> In determining the meaning of any Act of Congress, or of any ruling, regulation, or interpretation of the various administrative bureaus and agencies of the United States, the word "marriage" means only a legal union between one man and one woman as husband and wife, and the word "spouse" refers only to a person of the opposite sex who is a husband or a wife.

This provision controls over 1,000 federal laws whose coverage turns on marital status.

[Respondent Edith Windsor married Thea Spyer in Canada in 2007. The couple lived in New York, which recognized their marriage, until Spyer died in 2009. Spyer left her estate to Windsor but, because DOMA denied federal recognition to same-sex spouses, Windsor did not qualify for the marital exemption from the federal estate tax. Windsor was therefore compelled to pay $363,053, which she would not have owed if she had been married to a man.]

II

[In this section of the opinion, the Court holds that the case is properly before it. This holding is discussed in Chapter 1 F 2 of this Supplement.]

III

[It] seems fair to conclude that, until recent years, many citizens had not even considered the possibility that two persons of the same sex might aspire to occupy the same status and dignity as that of a man and woman in lawful marriage. For marriage between a man and a woman no doubt had been thought of by most people as essential to the very definition of that term and to its role and function throughout the history of civilization. That belief, for many who long have held it, became even more urgent, more cherished when challenged. For others, however, came the beginnings of a new perspective, a new insight. Accordingly some States concluded that same-sex marriage ought to be given recognition and validity in the law for those same-sex couples who wish to define themselves by their commitment to each other. The limitation of lawful marriage to heterosexual couples, which for centuries had been deemed both necessary and fundamental, came to be seen in New York and certain other States as an unjust exclusion. . . .

Against this background of lawful same-sex marriage in some States, the design, purpose, and effect of DOMA should be considered as the beginning point in deciding whether it is valid under the Constitution. By history and tradition the definition and regulation of marriage [has] been treated as being within the authority and realm of the separate States. Yet it is further established that Congress, in enacting discrete statutes, can make determinations that bear on marital rights and privileges. . . .

Though these discrete examples establish the constitutionality of limited federal laws that regulate the meaning of marriage in order to further federal policy, DOMA has a far greater reach; for it enacts a directive applicable to over 1,000 federal statutes and the whole realm of federal regulations. And its operation is directed to a class of persons that the laws of New York, and of 11 other States, have sought to protect. . . .

In order to assess the validity of that intervention it is necessary to discuss the extent of the state power and authority over marriage as a matter of history and tradition. State laws defining and regulating marriage, of course, must respect

VI. Implied Fundamental Rights

the constitutional rights of persons, see, *e.g.,* [*Loving v. Virginia*]; but, subject to those guarantees, "regulation of domestic relations" is "an area that has long been regarded as a virtually exclusive province of the States." . . .

Against this background DOMA rejects the long-established precept that the incidents, benefits, and obligations of marriage are uniform for all married couples within each State, though they may vary, subject to constitutional guarantees, from one State to the next. Despite these considerations, it is unnecessary to decide whether this federal intrusion on state power is a violation of the Constitution because it disrupts the federal balance. The State's power in defining the marital relation is of central relevance in this case quite apart from principles of federalism. Here the State's decision to give this class of persons the right to marry conferred upon them a dignity and status of immense import. When the State used its historic and essential authority to define the marital relation in this way, its role and its power in making the decision enhanced the recognition, dignity, and protection of the class in their own community. DOMA, because of its reach and extent, departs from this history and tradition of reliance on state law to define marriage. "'[D]iscriminations of an unusual character especially suggest careful consideration to determine whether they are obnoxious to the constitutional provision.'" [*Romer v. Evans.*]

The Federal Government uses this state-defined class for the opposite purpose—to impose restrictions and disabilities. That result requires this Court now to address whether the resulting injury and indignity is a deprivation of an essential part of the liberty protected by the Fifth Amendment. What the State of New York treats as alike the federal law deems unlike by a law designed to injure the same class the State seeks to protect. . . .

The States' interest in defining and regulating the marital relation, subject to constitutional guarantees, stems from the understanding that marriage is more than a routine classification for purposes of certain statutory benefits. Private, consensual sexual intimacy between two adult persons of the same sex may not be punished by the State, and it can form "but one element in a personal bond that is more enduring." [*Lawrence v. Texas.*] By its recognition of the validity of same-sex marriages performed in other jurisdictions and then by authorizing same-sex unions and same-sex marriages, New York sought to give further protection and dignity to that bond. For same-sex couples who wished to be married, the State acted to give their lawful conduct a lawful status. This status is a far-reaching legal acknowledgment of the intimate relationship between two people, a relationship deemed by the State worthy of dignity in the community equal with all other marriages. It reflects both the community's considered perspective on the historical roots of the institution of marriage and its evolving understanding of the meaning of equality.

IV

DOMA seeks to injure the very class New York seeks to protect. By doing so it violates basic due process and equal protection principles applicable to the Federal Government. See U.S. Const., Amdt. 5; Bolling v. Sharpe, 347 U.S. 497 (1954). The Constitution's guarantee of equality "must at the very least mean that a bare congressional desire to harm a politically unpopular group cannot" justify disparate treatment of that group. [*Department of Agriculture v. Marino.*] In determining whether a law is motived by an improper animus or purpose, "'[d]iscriminations of an unusual character'" especially require careful consideration. DOMA cannot survive under these principles. The responsibility of the States for the regulation of domestic relations is an important indicator of the substantial societal impact the State's classifications have in the daily lives and customs of its people. DOMA's unusual deviation from the usual tradition of recognizing and accepting state definitions of marriage here operates to deprive same-sex couples of the benefits and responsibilities that come with the federal recognition of their marriages. This is strong evidence of a law having the purpose and effect of disapproval of that class. The avowed purpose and practical effect of the law here in question are to impose a disadvantage, a separate status, and so a stigma upon all who enter into same-sex marriages made lawful by the unquestioned authority of the States.

The history of DOMA's enactment and its own text demonstrate that interference with the equal dignity of same-sex marriages, a dignity conferred by the States in the exercise of their sovereign power, was more than an incidental effect of the federal statute. It was its essence. The House Report announced its conclusion that "it is both appropriate and necessary for Congress to do what it can to defend the institution of traditional heterosexual marriage. . . . H.R. 3396 is appropriately entitled the 'Defense of Marriage Act.' The effort to redefine 'marriage' to extend to homosexual couples is a truly radical proposal that would fundamentally alter the institution of marriage." The House concluded that DOMA expresses "both moral disapproval of homosexuality, and a moral conviction that heterosexuality better comports with traditional (especially Judeo–Christian) morality." The stated purpose of the law was to promote an "interest in protecting the traditional moral teachings reflected in heterosexual-only marriage laws." Were there any doubt of this far-reaching purpose, the title of the Act confirms it: The Defense of Marriage. . . .

The Act's demonstrated purpose is to ensure that if any State decides to recognize same-sex marriages, those unions will be treated as second-class marriages for purposes of federal law. This raises a most serious question under the Constitution's Fifth Amendment.

DOMA's operation in practice confirms this purpose. When New York adopted a law to permit same-sex marriage, it sought to eliminate inequality; but DOMA

VI. Implied Fundamental Rights

frustrates that objective through a system-wide enactment with no identified connection to any particular area of federal law. DOMA writes inequality into the entire United States Code. The particular case at hand concerns the estate tax, but DOMA is more than a simple determination of what should or should not be allowed as an estate tax refund. Among the over 1,000 statutes and numerous federal regulations that DOMA controls are laws pertaining to Social Security, housing, taxes, criminal sanctions, copyright, and veterans' benefits.

DOMA's principal effect is to identify a subset of state-sanctioned marriages and make them unequal. The principal purpose is to impose inequality, not for other reasons like governmental efficiency. Responsibilities, as well as rights, enhance the dignity and integrity of the person. And DOMA contrives to deprive some couples married under the laws of their State, but not other couples, of both rights and responsibilities. By creating two contradictory marriage regimes within the same State, DOMA forces same-sex couples to live as married for the purpose of state law but unmarried for the purpose of federal law, thus diminishing the stability and predictability of basic personal relations the State has found it proper to acknowledge and protect. By this dynamic DOMA undermines both the public and private significance of state-sanctioned same-sex marriages; for it tells those couples, and all the world, that their otherwise valid marriages are unworthy of federal recognition. This places same-sex couples in an unstable position of being in a second-tier marriage. The differentiation demeans the couple, whose moral and sexual choices the Constitution protects, see Lawrence v. Texas, and whose relationship the State has sought to dignify. And it humiliates tens of thousands of children now being raised by same-sex couples. The law in question makes it even more difficult for the children to understand the integrity and closeness of their own family and its concord with other families in their community and in their daily lives.

Under DOMA, same-sex married couples have their lives burdened, by reason of government decree, in visible and public ways. By its great reach, DOMA touches many aspects of married and family life, from the mundane to the profound. It prevents same-sex married couples from obtaining government healthcare benefits they would otherwise receive. It deprives them of the Bankruptcy Code's special protections for domestic-support obligations. It forces them to follow a complicated procedure to file their state and federal taxes jointly.

For certain married couples, DOMA's unequal effects are even more serious. The federal penal code makes it a crime to "assaul[t], kidna[p], or murde[r] . . . a member of the immediate family" of "a United States official, a United States judge, [or] a Federal law enforcement officer," with the intent to influence or retaliate against that official. Although a "spouse" qualifies as a member of the officer's "immediate family," DOMA makes this protection inapplicable to same-sex spouses.

DOMA also brings financial harm to children of same-sex couples. It raises the cost of health care for families by taxing health benefits provided by employers to their workers' same-sex spouses. And it denies or reduces benefits allowed to families upon the loss of a spouse and parent, benefits that are an integral part of family security. DOMA divests married same-sex couples of the duties and responsibilities that are an essential part of married life and that they in most cases would be honored to accept were DOMA not in force. For instance, because it is expected that spouses will support each other as they pursue educational opportunities, federal law takes into consideration a spouse's income in calculating a student's federal financial aid eligibility. Same-sex married couples are exempt from this requirement. The same is true with respect to federal ethics rules. Federal executive and agency officials are prohibited from "participat[ing] personally and substantially" in matters as to which they or their spouses have a financial interest. [Under] DOMA, however, these Government-integrity rules do not apply to same-sex spouses....

The liberty protected by the Fifth Amendment's Due Process Clause contains within it the prohibition against denying to any person the equal protection of the laws. While the Fifth Amendment itself withdraws from Government the power to degrade or demean in the way this law does, the equal protection guarantee of the Fourteenth Amendment makes that Fifth Amendment right all the more specific and all the better understood and preserved.

The class to which DOMA directs its restrictions and restraints are those persons who are joined in same-sex marriages made lawful by the State. DOMA singles out a class of persons deemed by a State entitled to recognition and protection to enhance their own liberty. It imposes a disability on the class by refusing to acknowledge a status the State finds to be dignified and proper. DOMA instructs all federal officials, and indeed all persons with whom same-sex couples interact, including their own children, that their marriage is less worthy than the marriages of others. The federal statute is invalid, for no legitimate purpose overcomes the purpose and effect to disparage and to injure those whom the State, by its marriage laws, sought to protect in personhood and dignity. By seeking to displace this protection and treating those persons as living in marriages less respected than others, the federal statute is in violation of the Fifth Amendment. This opinion and its holding are confined to those lawful marriages.

The judgment of the Court of Appeals for the Second Circuit is affirmed.
It is so ordered.

CHIEF JUSTICE ROBERTS, dissenting.

[While] I disagree with the result to which the majority's analysis leads it in this case, I think it more important to point out that its analysis leads no further. The Court does not have before it, and the logic of its opinion does not decide, the distinct question whether the States, in the exercise of their "historic and essential authority to define the marital relation," may continue to utilize the traditional definition of marriage.

The majority goes out of its way to make this explicit in the penultimate sentence of its opinion. It states that "[t]his opinion and its holding are confined to those lawful marriages"—referring to same-sex marriages that a State has already recognized as a result of the local "community's considered perspective on the historical roots of the institution of marriage and its evolving understanding of the meaning of equality." Justice Scalia believes this is a "'bald, unreasoned disclaime[r].'" In my view, though, the disclaimer is a logical and necessary consequence of the argument the majority has chosen to adopt. The dominant theme of the majority opinion is that the Federal Government's intrusion into an area "central to state domestic relations law applicable to its residents and citizens" is sufficiently "unusual" to set off alarm bells. I think the majority goes off course, as I have said, but it is undeniable that its judgment is based on federalism. . . .

JUSTICE SCALIA, with whom JUSTICE THOMAS joins, and with whom [CHIEF JUSTICE ROBERTS] joins as to Part I, dissenting.

I

[In this portion of his dissent, Justice Scalia argues that the Court lacks jurisdiction over the case. This aspect of the dissent is discussed in Chapter 1 F 2 of this Supplement.

II . . .

B

As I have observed before, the Constitution does not forbid the government to enforce traditional moral and sexual norms. See Lawrence v. Texas (Scalia, J., dissenting). I will not swell the U.S. Reports with restatements of that point. It is enough to say that the Constitution neither requires nor forbids our society to approve of same-sex marriage, much as it neither requires nor forbids us to approve of no-fault divorce, polygamy, or the consumption of alcohol.

However, even setting aside traditional moral disapproval of same-sex marriage (or indeed same-sex sex), there are many perfectly valid—indeed, downright boring—justifying rationales for this legislation. Their existence ought to be the end of this case. For they give the lie to the Court's conclusion that only those with hateful hearts could have voted "aye" on this Act. And more importantly, they serve to make the contents of the legislators' hearts quite irrelevant: "It is a familiar principle of constitutional law that this Court will not strike down an otherwise constitutional statute on the basis of an alleged illicit legislative motive." [United States v. O'Brien, 391 U.S. 524 (1974)]. Or at least it *was* a familiar principle. By holding to the contrary, the majority has declared open season on any law that (in the opinion of the law's opponents and any panel of like-minded federal judges) can be characterized as mean-spirited.

The majority concludes that the only motive for this Act was the "bare . . . desire to harm a politically unpopular group." Bear in mind that the object of this condemnation is not the legislature of some once-Confederate Southern state (familiar objects of the Court's scorn), but our respected coordinate branches, the Congress and Presidency of the United States. Laying such a charge against them should require the most extraordinary evidence, and I would have thought that every attempt would be made to indulge a more anodyne explanation for the statute. . . .

To choose just one of these defenders' arguments, DOMA avoids difficult choice-of-law issues that will now arise absent a uniform federal definition of marriage. . . .

[The] majority says that the supporters of this Act acted with *malice*—with the *"purpose"* "to disparage and to injure" same-sex couples. It says that the motivation for DOMA was to "demean," to "impose inequality," to "impose . . . a stigma," to deny people "equal dignity," to brand gay people as "unworthy and to *"humiliat*[*e*]" their children (emphasis added).

I am sure these accusations are quite untrue. To be sure (as the majority points out), the legislation is called the Defense of Marriage Act. But to defend traditional marriage is not to condemn, demean, or humiliate those who would prefer other arrangements, any more than to defend the Constitution of the United States is to condemn, demean, or humiliate other constitutions. To hurl such accusations so casually demeans *this institution*. In the majority's judgment, any resistance to its holding is beyond the pale of reasoned disagreement. To question its highhanded invalidation of a presumptively valid statute is to act (the majority is sure) with *the purpose* to "disparage," "injure," "degrade," "demean," and "humiliate" our fellow human beings, our fellow citizens, who are homosexual. All that, simply for supporting an Act that did no more than codify an aspect of marriage that had been unquestioned in our society for most of its existence—indeed, had been unquestioned in virtually all societies for virtually all of human history. It is one thing for a society to elect change; it is another for a court of law to impose change by adjudging those who oppose it *hostes humani generis,* enemies of the human race.

* * *

The penultimate sentence of the majority's opinion is a naked declaration that "[t]his opinion and its holding are confined" to those couples "joined in same-sex marriages made lawful by the State." I have heard such "bald, unreasoned disclaimer[s]" before. [*Lawrence*]. When the Court declared a constitutional right to homosexual sodomy, we were assured that the case had nothing, nothing at all

VI. Implied Fundamental Rights

to do with "whether the government must give formal recognition to any relationship that homosexual persons seek to enter." Now we are told that DOMA is invalid because it "demeans the couple, whose moral and sexual choices the Constitution protects,"—with an accompanying citation of *Lawrence*. It takes real cheek for today's majority to assure us, as it is going out the door, that a constitutional requirement to give formal recognition to same-sex marriage is not at issue here—when what has preceded that assurance is a lecture on how superior the majority's moral judgment in favor of same-sex marriage is to the Congress's hateful moral judgment against it. I promise you this: The only thing that will "confine" the Court's holding is its sense of what it can get away with.

I do not mean to suggest disagreement with The Chief Justice's view, that lower federal courts and state courts can distinguish today's case when the issue before them is state denial of marital status to same-sex couples—or even that this Court could *theoretically* do so. Lord, an opinion with such scatter-shot rationales as this one (federalism noises among them) can be distinguished in many ways. And deserves to be. State and lower federal courts should take the Court at its word and distinguish away.

In my opinion, however, the view that *this* Court will take of state prohibition of same-sex marriage is indicated beyond mistaking by today's opinion. As I have said, the real rationale of today's opinion, whatever disappearing trail of its legalistic argle-bargle one chooses to follow, is that DOMA is motivated by "'bare . . . desire to harm'" couples in same-sex marriages. How easy it is, indeed how inevitable, to reach the same conclusion with regard to state laws denying same-sex couples marital status. Consider how easy (inevitable) it is to make the following substitutions in a passage from today's opinion:

> ~~DOMA's~~ *This state law's* principal effect is to identify a subset of ~~state-sanctioned marriages~~ *constitutionally protected sexual relationships*, see *Lawrence*, and make them unequal. The principal purpose is to impose inequality, not for other reasons like governmental efficiency. Responsibilities, as well as rights, enhance the dignity and integrity of the person. And ~~DOMA~~ *this state law* contrives to deprive some couples ~~married under the laws of their State~~ *enjoying constitutionally protected sexual relationships*, but not other couples, of both rights and responsibilities. . . .

Similarly transposable passages—deliberately transposable, I think—abound. In sum, that Court which finds it so horrific that Congress irrationally and hatefully robbed same-sex couples of the "personhood and dignity" which state legislatures conferred upon them, will of a certitude be similarly appalled by state legislatures' irrational and hateful failure to acknowledge that "personhood and dignity" in the first place. As far as this Court is concerned, no one should be fooled; it is just a matter of listening and waiting for the other shoe. . . .

[Few] public controversies touch an institution so central to the lives of so many, and few inspire such attendant passion by good people on all sides. Few public controversies will ever demonstrate so vividly the beauty of what our Framers gave us, a gift the Court pawns today to buy its stolen moment in the spotlight: a system of government that permits us to rule *ourselves*. Since DOMA's passage, citizens on all sides of the question have seen victories and they have seen defeats. There have been plebiscites, legislation, persuasion, and loud voices — in other words, democracy. Victories in one place for some, see North Carolina Const., Amdt. 1 (providing that "[m]arriage between one man and one woman is the only domestic legal union that shall be valid or recognized in this State") (approved by a popular vote, 61% to 39% on May 8, 2012), are offset by victories in other places for others, see Maryland Question 6 (establishing "that Maryland's civil marriage laws allow gay and lesbian couples to obtain a civil marriage license") (approved by a popular vote, 52% to 48%, on November 6, 2012). Even in a *single State,* the question has come out differently on different occasions. Compare Maine Question 1 (permitting "the State of Maine to issue marriage licenses to same-sex couples") (approved by a popular vote, 53% to 47%, on November 6, 2012) with Maine Question 1 (rejecting "the new law that lets same-sex couples marry") (approved by a popular vote, 53% to 47%, on November 3, 2009).

In the majority's telling, this story is black-and-white: Hate your neighbor or come along with us. The truth is more complicated. It is hard to admit that one's political opponents are not monsters, especially in a struggle like this one, and the challenge in the end proves more than today's Court can handle. Too bad. A reminder that disagreement over something so fundamental as marriage can still be politically legitimate would have been a fit task for what in earlier times was called the judicial temperament. We might have covered ourselves with honor today, by promising all sides of this debate that it was theirs to settle and that we would respect their resolution. We might have let the People decide.

But that the majority will not do. Some will rejoice in today's decision, and some will despair at it; that is the nature of a controversy that matters so much to so many. But the Court has cheated both sides, robbing the winners of an honest victory, and the losers of the peace that comes from a fair defeat. We owed both of them better. I dissent.

JUSTICE ALITO, with whom JUSTICE THOMAS joins as to Parts II and III, dissenting. . . .

I

[In this section of his opinion, Justice Alito argues that the case is properly before the Court. This part of the opinion is discussed in Chapter 1 F 2 of this Supplement.]

VI. Implied Fundamental Rights

II . . .

Same-sex marriage presents a highly emotional and important question of public policy—but not a difficult question of constitutional law. The Constitution does not guarantee the right to enter into a same-sex marriage. Indeed, no provision of the Constitution speaks to the issue.

The Court has sometimes found the Due Process Clauses to have a substantive component that guarantees liberties beyond the absence of physical restraint. And the Court's holding that "DOMA is unconstitutional as a deprivation of the liberty of the person protected by the Fifth Amendment of the Constitution," suggests that substantive due process may partially underlie the Court's decision today. But it is well established that any "substantive" component to the Due Process Clause protects only "those fundamental rights and liberties which are, objectively, 'deeply rooted in this Nation's history and tradition,'" Washington v. Glucksberg, as well as "'implicit in the concept of ordered liberty,' such that 'neither liberty nor justice would exist if they were sacrificed.'" *Glucksberg* (quoting Palko v. Connecticut).

It is beyond dispute that the right to same-sex marriage is not deeply rooted in this Nation's history and tradition. In this country, no State permitted same-sex marriage until the Massachusetts Supreme Judicial Court held in 2003 that limiting marriage to opposite-sex couples violated the State Constitution. Nor is the right to same-sex marriage deeply rooted in the traditions of other nations. No country allowed same-sex couples to marry until the Netherlands did so in 2000.

What Windsor and the United States seek, therefore, is not the protection of a deeply rooted right but the recognition of a very new right, and they seek this innovation not from a legislative body elected by the people, but from unelected judges. Faced with such a request, judges have cause for both caution and humility.

The family is an ancient and universal human institution. Family structure reflects the characteristics of a civilization, and changes in family structure and in the popular understanding of marriage and the family can have profound effects. Past changes in the understanding of marriage—for example, the gradual ascendance of the idea that romantic love is a prerequisite to marriage—have had far-reaching consequences. But the process by which such consequences come about is complex, involving the interaction of numerous factors, and tends to occur over an extended period of time.

We can expect something similar to take place if same-sex marriage becomes widely accepted. The long-term consequences of this change are not now known and are unlikely to be ascertainable for some time to come. There are those who think that allowing same-sex marriage will seriously undermine the institution of marriage. Others think that recognition of same-sex marriage will fortify a now-shaky institution.

At present, no one—including social scientists, philosophers, and historians—can predict with any certainty what the long-term ramifications of widespread acceptance of same-sex marriage will be. And judges are certainly not equipped to make such an assessment. The Members of this Court have the authority and the responsibility to interpret and apply the Constitution. Thus, if the Constitution contained a provision guaranteeing the right to marry a person of the same sex, it would be our duty to enforce that right. But the Constitution simply does not speak to the issue of same-sex marriage. In our system of government, ultimate sovereignty rests with the people, and the people have the right to control their own destiny. Any change on a question so fundamental should be made by the people through their elected officials.

III

Perhaps because they cannot show that same-sex marriage is a fundamental right under our Constitution, Windsor and the United States couch their arguments in equal protection terms. They argue that § 3 of DOMA discriminates on the basis of sexual orientation, that classifications based on sexual orientation should trigger a form of "heightened" scrutiny, and that § 3 cannot survive such scrutiny. They further maintain that the governmental interests that § 3 purports to serve are not sufficiently important and that it has not been adequately shown that § 3 serves those interests very well. The Court's holding, too, seems to rest on "the equal protection guarantee of the Fourteenth Amendment,"—although the Court is careful not to adopt most of Windsor's and the United States' argument.

In my view, the approach that Windsor and the United States advocate is misguided. Our equal protection framework, upon which Windsor and the United States rely, is a judicial construct that provides a useful mechanism for analyzing a certain universe of equal protection cases. But that framework is ill suited for use in evaluating the constitutionality of laws based on the traditional understanding of marriage, which fundamentally turn on what marriage is. . . .

In asking the Court to determine that § 3 of DOMA is subject to and violates heightened scrutiny, Windsor and the United States thus ask us to rule that the presence of two members of the opposite sex is as rationally related to marriage as white skin is to voting or a Y-chromosome is to the ability to administer an estate. That is a striking request and one that unelected judges should pause before granting. Acceptance of the argument would cast all those who cling to traditional beliefs about the nature of marriage in the role of bigots or superstitious fools.

By asking the Court to strike down DOMA as not satisfying some form of heightened scrutiny, Windsor and the United States are really seeking to have the Court resolve a debate between two competing views of marriage.

The first and older view, which I will call the "traditional" or "conjugal" view, sees marriage as an intrinsically opposite-sex institution. BLAG notes that

VI. Implied Fundamental Rights

virtually every culture, including many not influenced by the Abrahamic religions, has limited marriage to people of the opposite sex. And BLAG attempts to explain this phenomenon by arguing that the institution of marriage was created for the purpose of channeling heterosexual intercourse into a structure that supports child rearing. Others explain the basis for the institution in more philosophical terms. They argue that marriage is essentially the solemnizing of a comprehensive, exclusive, permanent union that is intrinsically ordered to producing new life, even if it does not always do so. While modern cultural changes have weakened the link between marriage and procreation in the popular mind, there is no doubt that, throughout human history and across many cultures, marriage has been viewed as an exclusively opposite-sex institution and as one inextricably linked to procreation and biological kinship.

The other, newer view is what I will call the "consent-based" vision of marriage, a vision that primarily defines marriage as the solemnization of mutual commitment—marked by strong emotional attachment and sexual attraction—between two persons. At least as it applies to heterosexual couples, this view of marriage now plays a very prominent role in the popular understanding of the institution. Indeed, our popular culture is infused with this understanding of marriage. Proponents of same-sex marriage argue that because gender differentiation is not relevant to this vision, the exclusion of same-sex couples from the institution of marriage is rank discrimination.

The Constitution does not codify either of these views of marriage (although I suspect it would have been hard at the time of the adoption of the Constitution or the Fifth Amendment to find Americans who did not take the traditional view for granted). The silence of the Constitution on this question should be enough to end the matter as far as the judiciary is concerned. Yet, Windsor and the United States implicitly ask us to endorse the consent-based view of marriage and to reject the traditional view, thereby arrogating to ourselves the power to decide a question that philosophers, historians, social scientists, and theologians are better qualified to explore. Because our constitutional order assigns the resolution of questions of this nature to the people, I would not presume to enshrine either vision of marriage in our constitutional jurisprudence. . . .

To the extent that the Court takes the position that the question of same-sex marriage should be resolved primarily at the state level, I wholeheartedly agree. I hope that the Court will ultimately permit the people of each State to decide this question for themselves. Unless the Court is willing to allow this to occur, the whiffs of federalism in the today's opinion of the Court will soon be scattered to the wind.

In any event, § 3 of DOMA, in my view, does not encroach on the prerogatives of the States, assuming of course that the many federal statutes affected by DOMA have not already done so. Section 3 does not prevent any State from recognizing same-sex marriage or from extending to same-sex couples any right, privilege, benefit, or obligation stemming from state law. All that § 3 does is to define a class of persons to whom federal law extends certain special benefits and upon whom federal law imposes certain special burdens. In these provisions, Congress used marital status as a way of defining this class—in part, I assume, because it viewed marriage as a valuable institution to be fostered and in part because it viewed married couples as comprising a unique type of economic unit that merits special regulatory treatment. Assuming that Congress has the power under the Constitution to enact the laws affected by § 3, Congress has the power to define the category of persons to whom those laws apply. . . .

H. The Contracts and Taking Clauses

Page 1003. At the end of section 3 of the Note, add the following:

Compare Arkansas Game & Fish Commission v. United States, ___ U.S. ___ 133 S. Ct. 511 (2012). The Commission owned a wildlife management area along the banks of the Black River, and regularly harvested timber in the reserve as part of its forest management efforts. One hundred fifteen miles upstream from the management area is the Clearwater Dam (the Dam), constructed by the United States Corps of Engineers in 1948. Shortly after constructing the Dam, the Corps adopted a Water Control Manual, which determined the rates at which water would be released from the Dam. In 1993, the Corps approved a planned deviation from the release rate in response to requests from farmers to provide for a longer harvest period. To reduce accumulation of water in the lake behind the Dam, the Corps extended the period in which a high amount of water would be released, resulting in flooding in the management area above historical norms. The flooding resulted in the destruction of timber in the management area and necessitated costly reclamation measures. Had the Corps released the water at a lower rate, the farmers would have had a shorter harvest season, but the timber would not have been damaged. The Court, in a unanimous decision written by Justice Ginsburg, held that government-induced flooding can amount to a taking even if it is temporary in duration.

If the Corps had not released the water, the farmers would have had a shorter harvest season. Why wouldn't this have been a taking? Suppose that the management area would have been flooded if the Dam had not been built in the first place. Would release of the extra water still be a taking? Would the result be different if the Corps built the Dam but then tore it down? If the initial Water Control Manual had provided for release of water at the higher rate?

Page 1011. At the end of section 1 of the Note, add the following:

Compare Koontz v. St. Johns River Water Management Dist., 570 U.S. ___ (2013). Petitioner owned a parcel of land that required state permits in order to develop. Petitioner suggested certain limitations on the development to mitigate the environmental damage, but the state Water Management District found these insufficient. Instead, the District proposed that petitioner either take further measures to mitigate the damage on his own property or that he hire contractors to make improvements on other property owned by the District. Petitioner refused to take these measures, and the District denied petitioner's application. Relying upon *Nollan,* Petitioner then filed suit in state court, but the Florida Supreme Court held that *Nollan* was distinguishable because there the state had approved an application on the condition that the land owner acceded to the state's demands, whereas here, the state had denied the application because he refused to make the concessions.

The United States Supreme Court, in a five-to-four decision, rejected this distinction and reversed the judgment below. Writing for the Court, Justice Alito stated that the principles undergirding *Nollan* "do not change depending on whether the government *approves* a permit on the condition that the applicant turn over property or *denies* a permit because the applicant refuses to do so. We have often concluded that denials of governmental benefits were impermissible under the unconstitutional conditions doctrine."

Neither party disputed the proposition that the District could have simply refused to grant the permit. How was petitioner made worse off by the District's suggestion of actions petitioner could take that would lead it to grant the permit? Consider in this regard Justice Alito's observation that "land-use permit applicants are especially vulnerable to the type of coercion that the unconstitutional conditions doctrine prohibits because the government often has broad discretion to deny a permit that is worth far more than property it would like to take." Compare the following observations in Justice Kagan's dissenting opinion:

> Consider the matter from the standpoint of the District's lawyer. The District, she learns, has found that [petitioner's] permit applications do not satisfy legal requirements. It can deny the permits on that basis; or it can suggest ways for [petitioner] to bring his application into compliance. If every suggestion could become the subject of a lawsuit under *Nollan,* [the] lawyer can give but one recommendation: Deny the permits without giving [petitioner] any advice—even if he asks for guidance. [Nothing] in the Takings Clause requires that folly.

Page 1011. At the end of section 2 of the Note, add the following:

Suppose instead of demanding a property interest to which it was otherwise not entitled, the state simply demands cash in return for a permit application. As noted above, in Koontz v. St. Johns River Water Management Dist., 570 U.S. ___ (2013), the District offered to allow petitioner to proceed with development if petitioner paid for improvements on a different parcel owned by the District. The Florida Supreme Court held that this situation was not governed by *Nollan* and *Dolan* because the requirement of a monetary payment did not constitute a "taking."

In his opinion for a five-to-four majority, Justice Alito rejected this reasoning: "[If] we accepted this argument it would be very easy for land-use permitting officials to evade the limitations of *Nollan* and *Dolan*. Because the government need only provide a permit applicant with one alternative that satisfies the nexus and rough proportionality standards, a permitting authority wishing to exact an easement could simply give the owner a choice of either surrendering an easement or making a payment equal to the easement's value."

The Court recognized that the takings clause does not apply to government-imposed financial obligations that do not operate upon or alter an identified property interest. Here, however, it found that the demand for money did operate upon such an interest "by directing the owner of a particular piece of property to make a monetary payment." The monetary obligation therefore "burdened petitioner's ownership of a specific parcel of land."

The Court acknowledged that neither a requirement that petitioner pay money to the state when not associated with a permit application nor the outright denial of a permit application would constitute a taking. How, then, can putting petitioner to a choice between these two options be a taking? Compare Rumsfeld v. FAIR, 547 U.S. 47 (2006), discussed in the main volume at page 1417. A federal statute provided that if a university denied access to military recruiters, it would lose access to federal funds. The Court, in a unanimous opinion written by Chief Justice Roberts, upheld the amendment on the ground that universities did not have a constitutional right either to the federal funds or to exclude the military. Are *Rumsfeld* and *Koontz* consistent?

Page 1013. At the end of section 4 of the Note, add the following:

Compare Arkansas Game & Fish Commission v. United States, ___ U.S. ___ 133 S. Ct. 511 (2012), where the Court, in a unanimous decision by Justice

VI. Implied Fundamental Rights

Ginsburg, held that government action producing temporary flooding of property can constitute a compensable taking. Although the Court held that there was "no automatic exemption from Takings Clause inspection," it also noted that whether there was in fact a taking depended on factors like the length of time that the area was flooded, the degree to which the invasion was intended or foreseeable, the character of the land, and the owner's reasonable investment-backed expectations regarding the land's use.

VII
FREEDOM OF EXPRESSION

A. Introduction

Page 1035. After section d of the Note, add the following:

e. R. Collins & D. Skover, On Dissent: Its Meaning in America 103, 115-116 (2013):

> [The First Amendment] safeguards the speech of those who refute our creeds, reject our values, renounce our government, and even repudiate our very way of life. This uniquely American principle of free speech provides a haven for irritating ranters and irksome rogues who feel the need to spoil our parade. In short, it protects the voice of the other. [In] one way or the other, the idea of dissent finds followers in every ideological camp. [As] Benjamin Franklin observed, "[i]t is the first responsibility of every citizen to question authority." [The] First Amendment sometimes converts illegal action into lawful action; it transforms what was seen as anarchy into what may be viewed as democratic engagement; and it reconfigures the relationship between society and its critics.

B. Content-Based Restrictions: Dangerous Ideas and Information

Page 1052. At the end of section 2 of the Note, add the following:

T. Healy, The Great Dissent: How Oliver Wendell Holmes Changed His Mind—and Changed the History of Free Speech in America 201, 343 (2013), provides a full account of Holmes's transformation. It began with a chance encounter with Learned Hand on a train in the summer of 1919. In the following months, Holmes came "under considerable pressure to rethink" his position. His opinions in *Schenck, Frohwerk,* and *Debs* were "attacked in the pages of the New Republic" by University of Chicago law professor Ernst Freund and in "the Harvard Law Review, challenged in correspondence with Learned Hand, confronted over tea by [Harvard law professor] Zechariah Chafee." The political theorist Harold Laski "fed him one book after another espousing a liberal view of free speech," and a young Felix Frankfurter "tried to arrange for him to write a piece on tolerance in the Atlantic Monthly." Although initially resistant to the criticism, Holmes came around. In 1922, Holmes confessed in a letter to Chafee that before the summer of 1919, when it came to issues of free speech and tolerance, "I was simply ignorant."

Page 1053. After section 5 of the Note, add the following:

5a. *"Sentences of twenty years imprisonment."* Holmes is clearly appalled that the defendants in *Abrams* were sentenced to terms "of twenty years imprisonment." He implies that the only plausible explanation for such severe punishment is that the defendants were being "made to suffer" not for any actual harm they might have caused to the nation (which he regards as trivial), but because of the government's hostility to their ideas (which he regards as impermissible). Suppose, then, that the defendants had been sentenced to a fine of $100 instead of to twenty years in prison. Should that have changed Holmes's analysis or the result? Should the nature or severity of the penalty be relevant to the constitutionality of a restriction of speech? See Coenen, Of Speech and Sanctions: Toward a Penalty-Sensitive Approach to the First Amendment, 112 Colum. L. Rev. 991 (2012).

Page 1070. After the long quotation from the opinion in *Yates*, add the following:

Harlan's opinion in *Yates* was greeted with puzzlement. One newspaper at the time characterized it as "a masterpiece of hair-splitting" and scholars characterized it as "complex, scholarly, and painfully dull" and as "a sort of *Finnegan's Wake* of impossibly nice distinctions." Nonetheless, "the Justice Department, faced with *Yates*'s insistence upon proof of advocacy to '*do* something, now or in the future, rather than merely to *believe* in something,' soon admitted that 'we cannot satisfy the evidentiary requirements laid down by the Supreme Court' and dismissed" all remaining Smith Act conspiracy cases then pending. R. Lichtman, The Supreme Court and McCarthy Era Repression: One Hundred Decisions 95-96 (2012).

Page 1078. Before the Note, add the following:

Consider also Tarkington, A First Amendment Theory for Protecting Attorney Speech, 45 U.C. Davis L. Rev. 27, 79 (2011):

> The "material support" statute in *Humanitarian Law Project* not only *frustrates* the attorney-client relationship [but] in fact *criminalizes* [it] and imputes culpability for the client's unlawful conduct onto the advising attorney. As with Red Scare statutes aimed at eradicating communism, the "material support" statute, as applied to the plaintiffs, can be said to "quite literally establish[] guilt by association alone" because it criminalizes association even if the associating attorney "disagree[s] with th[e] unlawful aims of the [organization]."

Page 1100. At the end of *Snyder v. Phelps*, add the following:

Suppose a gay teenager dies in a car accident and the members of the Westboro Baptist Church picket his funeral. Suppose further that their speech is directed specifically at the parents of the boy, rather than at the general public. Their signs charge that the son died because he was gay, condemn the parents for failing to "correct" their son's homosexuality, and blame them for his death. Would the case be any different? See Heyman, To Drink the Cup of Fury: Funeral Picketing, Public Discourse, and the First Amendment, 45 Conn. L. Rev. 101 (2012). In the years since *Snyder*, many states have enacted "buffer-zone" laws that prohibit any picketing within a certain distance of a funeral within a certain time before and after the funeral. Are such laws constitutional? See Heyman, supra, at 164-172.

Page 1112. After section 8 of the Note, add the following:

9. *Facts and the First Amendment*. Note that in many cases the government is attempting to restrict the dissemination of facts rather than opinions. The seminal conception of the First Amendment was about the "marketplace of ideas." How do facts fit into this marketplace? Should government efforts to restrict the dissemination of facts be treated the same way as government efforts to restrict the dissemination of ideas? In addition to the cases in this section, consider also

the following: (a) an anti-abortion group publishes on its website the names and addresses of abortion providers; (b) a newspaper publishes the name of a rape victim; (c) a reporter discloses the names of covert American agents in Iran. See Bhagwat, Details: Specific Facts and the First Amendment, 86 S. Cal. L. Rev. 1 (2012).

D. Content-Based Restrictions: "Low" Value

Page 1149. At the end of section c of the Note, add the following:

Ashdown, Distorting Democracy: Campaign Lies in the 21st Century, 20 Wm. & Mary Bill Rts. J. 1085 (2012).

Page 1173. At the end of section 1c of the Note, add the following:

Consider also Stone, Ronald Coase's First Amendment, 54 J. Law & Econ. 367, 374 (2011):

> As both logic and history teach, the temptation of public officials to use government power to stifle criticism and distort public debate poses a direct threat to the very existence of a self-governing society. Such behavior not only gives those in power a continuing political advantage over their challengers but also enables them to prevent any criticism or even discussion of their actions. It therefore freezes policies in place. In the sphere of economic regulation, however, that is not the case. As long as free speech is guaranteed, even an inefficient and rent-seeking economic regulation can be publicly criticized and ultimately changed. From a constitutional standpoint, economic freedom simply does not stand on the same footing as freedom of speech.

Page 1173. After section 1e of the Note, add the following:

f. Brudney, The First Amendment and Commercial Advertising, 53 B.C. L. Rev. 1153, 1179, 1168 (2013):

It has been suggested that because it is speech and serves a communicative function, commercial speech is entitled to the same protection against government regulation as other protected [speech]. As a predicate for First Amendment protection, however, commercial speech's communicative function may not be sufficient to justify such protection. . . .

[This is so because,] in much commercial speech, the speaker's concern is primarily, or only, with the choices to be made by individual consumers for their personal benefit, rather than for the benefit of society as a whole. The question that each consumer is presumed to ask in making his choice is: "What is good, or best, for me?" [But in the case of traditionally protected speech,] the question the addressee or member of the audience is presumed to ask is: "What is good, or best, for the community or society?" Such an inquiry is not of central concern to the speaker-seller or indeed to the listener-buyer [in the context of commercial speech]. . . .

Page 1180. At the end of section 3 of the Note, add the following:

Is the Court's concern with paternalism in these cases warranted? Consider Brudney, The First Amendment and Commercial Speech, 53 B.C. L. Rev. 1153, 1194-1197 (2013):

Prohibiting or regulating truthful commercial communications about lawful activities that may be of interest to the listener is said to be especially objectionable interference, in that it paternalistically precludes the listener from knowledgeably deciding whether to risk or incur such harm. [In effect, such paternalism interferes with the consumer's ability to make] a possibly harmful choice to satisfy a preference in personal matters [because] the government believes satisfying that preference to be harmful to him or her, as well as to others. . . .

The predicate on which the charge of paternalism rests (the consumers' ability to "perceive their own best interests . . . if they are well enough informed," and to act upon that perception) assumes an apperceptive base of relevant information and knowledge. In the universe of retail mass marketing, the billions of dollars spent by sellers in the aggregate to acculturate consumers to desire products or services that may (or may not) create unspecified long-term health or safety problems, or other costs, are expenditures that are not offset (and are not likely to be offset without government regulation) by reasonably comparable nongovernmental expenditures for educative "debiasing" efforts.

It is that background, structured by government-created property rules in a market economy, that enables sellers or offerors to shape consumer tastes and preferences so as to affect a consumer's "free" choice in responding to offers. It also raises the question: Which government intervention is, or would be, "paternalistic?" Was the consumer's relevant knowledge for making a choice enhanced by the Court's constitutionally rejecting Virginia's prohibition of price advertisements for prescription drugs? Or was it enhanced by Virginia forbidding such ads? Either way, the government's intervention to enable the consumer "freely" to determine her own best interests is (or is not) "paternalism."

Page 1201. After section 9 of the Note, add the following:

10. *Obscenity and substantive due process.* Even if obscenity is not protected by the First Amendment, is it protected from prohibition by the doctrine of substantive due process, as articulated in such decisions as *Griswold v. Connecticut, Roe v. Wade, Planned Parenthood v. Casey,* and *Lawrence v. Texas,* supra section VI F? In *Lawrence*, the Court observed that "liberty gives substantial protection to adult persons in deciding how to conduct their private lives in matters pertaining to sex." Does "the right of autonomous decision-making" in private matters include "the protection of both intimate sexual conduct and the commercial transactions that enable and promote sexual intimacy"? Kinsley, Sexual Privacy in the Internet Age: How Substantive Due Process Protects Online Obscenity, 16 Vand. J. Ent. & Tech. L. ___ (2013). See Reliable Consultants, Inc. v. Earle, 517 F.3d 738 (5th Cir. 2008) (invalidating on substantive due process grounds a Texas law prohibiting any person to sell, advertise, give away or lend any device "designed or marketed for sexual stimulation").

Page 1211. At the end of *United States v. Stevens*, add the following:

Within months of the Supreme Court's decision in *Stevens,* Congress amended § 48. The new provision, titled "Animal crush videos," defines an "animal crush video" as "any photograph, motion-picture film, video or digital recording, or electronic image" that (1) "depicts actual conduct in which one or more living non-human mammals, birds, reptiles, or amphibians is intentionally crushed, burned, drowned, suffocated, impaled or otherwise subjected to serious bodily injury" and (2) "is obscene." The statute exempts any visual depiction of "customary and normal veterinary or agricultural husbandry practices," "the slaughter of

VII. Freedom of Expression   Page 1263

animals for food," or "hunting, trapping or fishing." Is this statute constitutional? See United States v. Ashley Nicole Richards and Brent Justice, ___ F. Supp. ___ (S.D. Tex. 2013) (holding that the revised statute violates the First Amendment).

Page 1214. At the end of *Brown v. Entertainment Merchants Association*, add the following:

Consider Schauer, Harm(s) and the First Amendment, 2011 Sup. Ct. Rev. 81, 108, 110:

> *Stevens*, *Snyder*, and *Entertainment Merchants* all involved moderately clear harms—to animals, to grieving parents, and [to] potential victims of the aggressiveness of teenagers. [The] First Amendment, as much if not more than the rest of the Constitution, is a mandate to the courts to engage in a common law process of developing the rules, principles, standards, maxims, canons, and precedents that together produce what we call legal doctrine. But in considering the common law nature of that development of First Amendment doctrine, it is important to bear in mind Lord Mansfield's optimistic assessment that the common law "works itself pure." In light of [this] aspiration, it is often appropriate to ask whether the progression of time, the increase in the stock of examples, and the continued testing of provisional rules and principles has produced improvement. . . .

Do you agree with Schauer that "one of the surprising things about *Stevens*, *Snyder*, and *Entertainment Merchants*, taken as a group, is that they give little cause for optimism about the continuing refinement of First Amendment doctrine"?

E. *Content-Neutral Restrictions*

Page 1263. At the end of the Note, add the following:

How has the Roberts Court interpreted and applied the *Chaplinsky* dictum? In the decades after *Chaplinsky*, defenders of free speech viewed the *Chaplinsky* dictum as an "unfortunate" invitation to the Court to make open-ended value judgments about which speech is and is not to be protected by the First Amendment. Indeed, Harry Kalven criticized it in the early 1970s as a "broad dictum" that "haunted constitutional law." H. Kalven, A Worthy Tradition: Freedom of

Speech in America 18 (1988). In light of the Roberts Court's decisions in *Stevens, Snyder, Brown,* and *Alvarez,* however, the *Chaplinsky* dictum seems to have taken on a somewhat different cast. Consider Collins, Exceptional Freedom: The Roberts Court, the First Amendment, and the New Absolutism, 76 Alb. L. Rev. 409, 424 (2013):

> [The Roberts Court] has shown no signs of moving away from the jurisprudence of its predecessors in diminishing the domain of *Chaplinsky*'s original exceptions. (For example, pre-Roberts Courts have held that defamation is not entirely unprotected, and lewd and profane speech is sometimes protected.) Moreover, the current Court has generally declined to expressly invoke *Chaplinsky*'s low value [doctrine] as a rationale for enlarging the realm of unprotected expression. In fact, the Court seems to have moved in the opposite direction. [While] some earlier Courts relied on *Chaplinsky*'s two-level theory to cabin free speech protection [citing *Roth*], the Roberts Court has sometimes taken an entirely different approach, one that expands the domain of protected speech. In doing so, it has produced an exceptional kind of freedom in which [speech is] categorically protected unless [it is] among the designated kinds of expression definitely exempted from First Amendment protection.

Page 1334. At the end of section 3 of the Note, add the following:

Are there circumstances in which the government's own speech might violate the establishment clause? The equal protection clause? See Norton, The Equal Protection Implications of Government's Hateful Speech, 54 Wm. & Mary L. Rev. 159 (2012).

Page 1337. At the end of the Note on Government Speech, add the following:

AGENCY FOR INTERNATIONAL DEVELOPMENT v. ALLIANCE FOR OPEN SOCIETY INTERNATIONAL, ___ U.S. ___ **(2013).** The United States Leadership Against HIV/AIDS, Tuberculosis, and Malaria Act of 2003 (Leadership Act) authorized the appropriation of billions of dollars to fund efforts by nongovernmental organizations to combat HIV/AIDS worldwide. The Act imposed a condition ("The Policy Requirement") on all recipients of funds under

VII. Freedom of Expression

the Act: all recipients must explicitly oppose prostitution. This requirement was challenged by recipients of Leadership Act funds who wish to remain neutral on the issue of prostitution. The Court, in a six-to-two decision, held that this requirement violated the First Amendment rights of recipients.

Chief Justice Roberts delivered the opinion of the Court: "The Policy Requirement mandates that recipients of Leadership Act funds explicitly agree with the Government's policy to oppose prostitution. . . . It is, however, a basic First Amendment principle that 'freedom of speech prohibits the government from telling people what they must say.' [Citing *West Virginia Bd. of Ed. v. Barnette*, main volume page 1416; *Wooley v. Maynard*, main volume page 1416]. [Were The Policy Requirement] enacted as a direct regulation of speech, [it] would plainly violate the First Amendment. The question is whether the Government may nonetheless impose that requirement as a condition on the receipt of federal funds. . . .

"[As] a general matter, if a party objects to a condition on the receipt of federal funding, its recourse is to decline the funds. This remains true when the objection is that a condition may affect the recipient's exercise of its First Amendment rights. [Citing *United States v. American Library Ass'n*.] At the same time, however, we have held that the Government 'may not deny a benefit to a person on a basis that infringes his constitutionally protected . . . freedom of speech even if he has no entitlement to that benefit.' In some cases, a funding condition can result in an unconstitutional burden on First Amendment rights. . . .

"The dissent thinks that can only be true when the condition is not relevant to the objectives of the program [or] when the condition is actually coercive, in the sense of an offer that cannot be refused. Our precedents, however, are not so limited. In the present context, the relevant distinction that has emerged from our cases is between conditions that define the limits of the government spending program—those that specify the activities Congress wants to subsidize—and conditions that seek to leverage funding to regulate speech outside the contours of the program itself. The line is hardly clear, in part because the definition of a particular program can always be manipulated to subsume the challenged condition. We have held, however, that 'Congress cannot recast a condition on funding as a mere definition of its program in every case, lest the First Amendment be reduced to a simple semantic exercise.'" [*Velazquez*.]

As an example, Chief Justice Roberts invoked *FCC v. League of Women Voters*, in which "the Court struck down a condition on federal financial assistance to noncommercial broadcast television and radio stations that prohibited all editorializing, including with private funds. Even a station receiving only one percent of its overall budget from the Federal Government, the Court explained, was 'barred absolutely from all editorializing.' [The] law provided no way for a station to limit its use of federal funds to noneditorializing activities, while using private funds 'to make known its views on matters of public importance.' The prohibition thus went beyond ensuring that federal funds not be used to subsidize 'public broadcasting station editorials,' and instead leveraged the federal funding to regulate the stations' speech outside the scope of the program.

"Our decision in *Rust* elaborated on the approach [in] *League of Women Voters*. In *Rust*, [the] organizations received funds from a variety of sources other than the Federal Government for a variety of purposes. The Act, however, prohibited the Title X federal funds from being 'used in programs where abortion is a method of family planning.' To enforce this provision, HHS regulations barred Title X projects from advocating abortion as a method of family planning, and required grantees to ensure that their Title X projects were 'physically and financially separate' from their other projects that engaged in the prohibited activities. . . .

"We explained that Congress can, without offending the Constitution, selectively fund certain programs to address an issue of public concern, without funding alternative ways of addressing the same problem. In Title X, Congress had defined the federal program to encourage only particular family planning methods. The challenged regulations were simply 'designed to ensure that the limits of the federal program are observed,' and 'that public funds [are] spent for the purposes for which they were authorized.' [The] regulations governed only the scope of the grantee's Title X projects, leaving it 'unfettered in its other activities.' [Title X grantees could continue to engage in abortion advocacy as long as they conducted] 'those activities through programs that are separate and independent from the project that receives Title X funds.' Because the regulations did not 'prohibit[ ] the recipient from engaging in the protected conduct outside the scope of the federally funded program,' they did not run afoul of the First Amendment. Here, however, [the] Policy Requirement falls on the unconstitutional side of the line. [By] demanding that funding recipients adopt—as their own—the Government's view on an issue of public concern, the condition by its very nature affects 'protected conduct outside the scope of the federally funded program.' [By] requiring recipients to profess a specific belief, the Policy Requirement goes beyond defining the limits of the federally funded program to defining the recipient. . . .

"The Government suggests that the Policy Requirement is necessary because, without it, the grant of federal funds could free a recipient's private funds 'to be used to promote prostitution.' [Citing *Holder v. Humanitarian Law Project*.] That argument assumes that federal funding will simply supplant private funding, rather than pay for new programs or expand existing ones. The Government offers no support for that assumption as a general matter, or any reason to believe it is true here. And if the Government's argument were correct, *League of Women Voters* would have come out differently, and much of the reasoning [of] *Rust* would have been beside the point.

"The Government cites but one case to support that argument, *Holder v. Humanitarian Law Project*. That case concerned the quite different context of

VII. Freedom of Expression

a ban on providing material support to terrorist organizations, where the record indicated that support for those organizations' nonviolent operations was funneled to support their violent activities.

"Pressing its argument further, the Government contends that 'if organizations awarded federal funds to implement Leadership Act programs could at the same time promote or affirmatively condone prostitution or sex trafficking, whether using public *or private* funds, it would undermine the government's program and confuse its message opposing prostitution.' But the Policy Requirement goes beyond preventing recipients from using private funds in a way that would undermine the federal program. It requires them to pledge allegiance to the Government's policy of eradicating prostitution. As to that, we cannot improve upon what Justice Jackson wrote for the Court 70 years ago: 'If there is any fixed star in our constitutional constellation, it is that no official, high or petty, can prescribe what shall be orthodox in politics, nationalism, religion, or other matters of opinion or force citizens to confess by word or act their faith therein.' [Quoting *West Virginia Board of Education v. Barnette*.]

"The Policy Requirement compels as a condition of federal funding the affirmation of a belief that by its nature cannot be confined within the scope of the Government program. In so doing, it violates the First Amendment and cannot be sustained."

Justice Scalia, joined by Justice Thomas, dissented: "The First Amendment does not mandate a viewpoint neutral government. Government must choose between rival ideas and adopt some as its own: competition over cartels, solar energy over coal, weapon development over disarmament, and so forth. Moreover, the government may enlist the assistance of those who believe in its ideas to carry them to fruition; and it need not enlist for that purpose those who oppose or do not support the ideas. That seems to me a matter of the most common common sense. . . .

"The argument is that this commonsense principle will enable the government to discriminate against, and injure, points of view to which it is opposed. Of course the Constitution does not prohibit government spending that discriminates against, and injures, points of view to which the government is opposed; every government program which takes a position on a controversial issue does that. Anti-smoking programs injure cigar aficionados, programs encouraging sexual abstinence injure free-love advocates, etc. The constitutional prohibition at issue here is not a prohibition against discriminating against or injuring opposing points of view, but the First Amendment's prohibition against the coercing of speech. I am frankly dubious that a condition for eligibility to participate in a minor federal program such as this one runs afoul of that prohibition even when the condition is irrelevant to the goals of the program. Not every disadvantage is a coercion.

"But that is not the issue before us here. Here the views that the Government demands an applicant forswear—or that the Government insists an applicant favor—are relevant to the program in question. The program is valid only if the Government is entitled to disfavor the opposing view (here, advocacy of or toleration of prostitution). And if the program can disfavor it, so can the selection of those who are to administer the program. There is no risk that this principle will enable the Government to discriminate arbitrarily against positions it disfavors. It would not, for example, permit the Government to exclude from bidding on defense contracts anyone who refuses to abjure prostitution. But here a central part of the Government's HIV/AIDS strategy is the suppression of prostitution, by which HIV is transmitted. It is entirely reasonable to admit to participation in the program only those who believe in that goal. . . .

"Of course the most obvious manner in which the admission to a program of an ideological opponent can frustrate the purpose of the program is by freeing up the opponent's funds for use in its ideological opposition. [Money] is fungible. The economic reality is that when NGOs can conduct their AIDS work on the Government's dime, they can expend greater resources on policies that undercut the Leadership Act. The Government need not establish by record evidence that this will happen. To make it a valid consideration in determining participation in federal programs, it suffices that this is a real and obvious risk. [In] *FCC v. League of Women Voters,* the ban on editorializing [was] disallowed precisely because it did not further a relevant, permissible policy of the Federal Communications Act. . . .

"The majority cannot credibly say that this speech condition is coercive, so it does not. It pussyfoots around the lack of coercion by invalidating the Leadership Act for '*requiring* recipients to profess a specific belief' and "*demanding* that funding recipients adopt—as their own—the Government's view on an issue of public concern.' But like King Cnut's commanding of the tides, here the Government's 'requiring' and 'demanding' have no coercive effect. In the end, and in the circumstances of this case, [there] is no compulsion at all. It is the reasonable price of admission to a limited government-spending program that each organization remains free to accept or reject. . . ."

Page 1418. After section 5 of the Note, add the following:

5a. *Conditions on recipients of public funds.* See Agency for International Development v. Alliance for Open Society International, ___ U.S. ___ (2013), 133 S. Ct. 2321 (2013), insert in this Supplement for page 1337 of the main volume.

VII. Freedom of Expression

F. Freedom of the Press

Page 1426. After section 2 of the Note, add the following:

2a. *Protecting the anonymity of the source.* Instead of focusing on the First Amendment right of the reporter to keep sources confidential, would it make more sense to focus on the First Amendment right of the source to engage in anonymous speech? After all, in a series of decisions, including *Talley v. California*, *McIntyre v. Ohio Elections Commission*, *NAACP v. Alabama*, and *Brown v. Socialist Workers*, the Court has protected a right to anonymous speech, noting that anonymous speech has "played an important role in the progress of mankind" and that "persecuted groups" throughout history "have been able to criticize oppressive practices either anonymously or not at all." Consider Jones, Re-Thinking Reporter's Privilege, 111 Mich. L. Rev. 1221 (2013):

> A confidential source who does not wish to have her name revealed is analytically indistinguishable from any other author, writer, or speaker who wishes to convey information anonymously. Like the leafleteer in *Talley* . . . and the concerned taxpayer in *McIntyre*, . . . a confidential source offers information that she wishes to make public without attribution . . . for any number of reasons that the Court has acknowledged as valid. [The] source should be entitled to protection under the anonymous speech doctrine for statements made to a reporter in confidence.

2b. *Investigative journalism or criminal solicitation?* Suppose a reporter persuades a public employee unlawfully to leak classified information. Can the reporter constitutionally be convicted of the crime of criminal solicitation? Recall *O'Brien*. Suppose a journalist conducts an illegal wiretap in order to prove that a congressman took a bribe. Would her conduct be protected by the First Amendment? If not, is criminal solicitation any different? See G. Stone, Top Secret: When Government Keeps Us in the Dark 29-38 (2007) (arguing that because prosecution of journalists for the crime of solicitation would interject "government into the very heart of the journalist-source relationship" and thus "have a serious chilling effect" on legitimate and important journalist-source exchanges, the government should not be able to punish journalists for encouraging public employees to disclose classified information unless the journalist (a) expressly incites the leak and (b) knows that publication of the information would likely cause imminent and grave harm to the national security). Can that position be reconciled with the wiretap example or with *Branzburg*?

VIII
THE CONSTITUTION AND RELIGION

A. *Introduction: Historical and Analytical Overview*

Page 1467. **At the end of section 9 of the Note, add the following:**

Schwartzman, What If Religion Is Not Special?, 79 U. Chi. L. Rev. 1351 (2012), argues that

> [many] of the most widely held normative justifications for favoring (or disfavoring) religion are prone to predictable forms of internal incoherence [and] accounts [that] manage to avoid such incoherence succeed only at the cost of committing other serious errors, especially in allowing various types of unfairness toward religious believers, nonbelievers, or both. The upshot of all this is that principles of disestablishment and free exercise ought to be conceived in terms that go beyond the category of religion. Instead of disabling or protecting only religious beliefs and practices, the law ought to provide similar treatment for comparable secular ethical, moral, and philosophical views.

IX
STATE ACTION, BASELINES, AND THE PROBLEM OF PRIVATE POWER

E. *Unconstitutional Conditions and the Benefit/Burden Distinction*

Page 1613. At the bottom of the page, add the following:

The Court elaborated on its *Nollan* holding in Koontz v. St. Johns River Water Management Dist., 570 U.S. ___ (2013), where it held that the same principle was applicable when, instead of accepting the condition, as the landowner had in *Nollan,* the landholder rejected the condition leading to the denial of a permit. Writing for five justices, Justice Alito stated:

> Our decisions [reflect] two realities of the permitting process. The first is that land-use permit applicants are especially vulnerable to the type of coercion that the unconstitutional conditions doctrine prohibits because the government often has broad discretion to deny a permit that is worth far more than property it would like to take. By conditioning a building permit on the owner's deeding over a public right-of-way, for example, the government can pressure an owner into voluntarily giving up property for which the Fifth Amendment would otherwise require just compensation. So long as the building permit is more valuable than any just compensation the owner could hope to receive for the right-of-way, the owner is likely to

accede to the government's demand no matter how unreasonable. Extortionate demands of this sort frustrate the Fifth Amendment right to just compensation, and the unconstitutional conditions doctrine prohibits them.

The second reality of the permitting process is that many proposed land uses threaten to impose costs on the public that dedications of property can offset. [Insisting] that landowners internalize the negative externalities of their conduct is a hallmark of responsible land-use policy, and we have long sustained such regulations against constitutional attack.

Nollan [accommodates] both realities by allowing the government to condition approval of a permit on the dedication of property to the public so long as there is a "nexus" and "rough proportionality" between the property the government demands and the social costs of the applicant's proposal. Our precedents thus enable permitting authorities to insist that applicants bear the full costs of their proposals while still forbidding the government from engaging in "out-and-out . . . extortion" that would thwart the Fifth Amendment right to just compensation.

Page 1620. At the end of the Note, add the following:

(f) For an interesting unconstitutional conditions decision, see Agency for International Development v. Alliance for Open Society International, ___ U.S. ___, 133 S. Ct. 2321 (2013). By statute, Congress authorized the appropriation of billions of dollars to fund efforts by nongovernmental organizations to combat HIV/AIDS worldwide. Congress also imposed two conditions on the receipt of funds: (1) no funds "may be used to promote or advocate the legalization or practice of prostitution"; and (2) no funds may be used by an organization "that does not have a policy explicitly opposing prostitution."

The Court struck down the second condition. It emphasized a distinction between two kinds of conditions: (1) those that define the limits of the Government spending program (specifying the activities Congress wants to subsidize) and (2) those that seek to leverage funding to regulate speech outside the contours of the federal program itself. While Congress may limit its own spending, so that cases that fall within category (1) are permissible, Congress faces constitutional limits when it restricts speech in category (2).

The Court held that the restriction at issue fell in the second category: "By demanding that funding recipients adopt—as their own—the Government's view on an issue of public concern, the condition by its very nature affects 'protected conduct outside the scope of the federally funded program.' By requiring recipients to profess a specific belief, the [requirement] goes beyond defining the limits of the federally funded program to defining the recipient." In the Court's

IX. State Action, Baselines, and the Problem of Private Power

view, the requirement "goes beyond preventing recipients from using private funds in a way that would undermine the federal program. It requires them to pledge allegiance to the Government's policy of eradicating prostitution."

Justice Scalia, joined by Justice Thomas, dissented. He contended that the requirement at issue "is nothing more than a means of selecting suitable agents to implement the Government's chosen strategy to eradicate HIV/AIDS. That is perfectly permissible under the Constitution." In his view, "the government may enlist the assistance of those who believe in its ideas to carry them to fruition; and it need not enlist for that purpose those who oppose or do not support the ideas. That seems to me a matter of the most common common sense. For example: One of the purposes of America's foreign-aid programs is the fostering of goodwill towards this country. If the organization Hamas—reputed to have an efficient system for delivering welfare—were excluded from a program for the distribution of U.S. food assistance, no one could reasonably object. And that would remain true if Hamas were an organization of United States citizens entitled to the protection of the Constitution. [And] the same is true when the rejected organization is not affirmatively opposed to, but merely unsupportive of, the object of the federal program, which appears to be the case here. (Respondents do not promote prostitution, but neither do they wish to oppose it.) A federal program to encourage healthy eating habits need not be administered by the American Gourmet Society, which has nothing against healthy food but does not insist upon it."

Made in the USA
Lexington, KY
08 January 2014